HOLIDAY HUMOR

pil
Publications International, Ltd.

Written by Lisa Brooks

Photography from Shutterstock.com, Library of Congress

Louis Weber, CEO
Publications International, Ltd.
8140 Lehigh Avenue
Morton Grove, IL 60053

ISBN: 978-1-68022-971-4

Manufactured in Canada.

8 7 6 5 4 3 2 1

Table of Contents

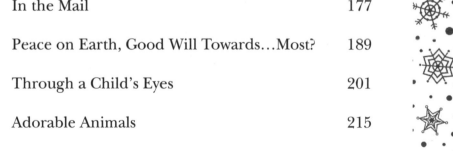

Introduction

It's beginning to look a lot like Christmas! Celebrate the season with joy and laughter—and if you need a little help achieving those, then *Holiday Humor* is the book for you. Here you'll find jokes, amusing stories, song parodies, cartoons, and goofy photographs to make you grin, giggle, and guffaw.

The Man in Red

With his boisterous laugh, his twinkling eyes, and his affinity for cookies, Santa is a staple of Christmas. In this chapter, you'll find some jolly stories and cartoons that celebrate the man of the season.

Whiskers and a Soft Stomach

Santa's presence in our lives can be tracked in four stages:

1) When you're young, you believe in Santa.

2) As a young adult, you don't believe in Santa.

3) As an adult, you pretend to be Santa for the kids in your life.

4) Once you're old, you look like Santa without even trying!

"Today's speaker is an expert on distribution."

Could He or Couldn't He?

Have you ever doubted that Santa Claus could really travel around the world, deliver presents, eat the snacks left out for him, and then move on undetected—all in a single night? Well, astrophysicist Ethan Siegel did the math, and it turns out that Santa's seemingly impossible feats aren't beyond the realm of reality!

In order to zoom around the world and hit each house, Santa would need to travel at about 6,400 miles per hour. According to Siegel, although this sounds far too fast, it's only a quarter as fast as most rockets go. So there are, in fact, vehicles that travel faster than Santa needs to go!

Siegel also points out that all those cookies and milk left for Santa are perfect for converting into fuel, using Einstein's $E=mc^2$ equation. And he suggests that perhaps Santa's elves are also proficient in engineering, possibly creating robot arms and pressurized suits to help the big man with his tasks.

You never know—after all, he is Santa!

Dear Santa,
define "good"

All modern inventions make their way to the
North Pole, including the assembly line.

Ho Ho Ho

Question: Why is Christmas like a day at the office?

Answer: Because you do all the work, and the fat guy in the suit gets all the credit!

Santa by the Numbers

Santa Claus undertakes quite a feat every year: he oversees toy production at his workshop, hauls everything around the world, and delivers every present in time for Christmas morning—and it's all free for us, the recipients of his generosity. So have you ever wondered how much it costs to give everyone in the world a merry Christmas?

Quora user Kynan Eng, who is a research specialist, ran some figures and discovered that the jolly old man would need quite a large savings account to accomplish his seasonal goals.

Take toy production: there are approximately 2.43 billion kids in the world, so if Santa spends just $10 per child to make toys, package them, and wrap them, that's $24.3 billion just for toys.

But the most expensive part of Santa's holiday operation is the shipping. In order to ship millions of tons of presents around the world, it would cost about $95.8 billion!

Fortunately, Santa doesn't need money—just holiday magic!

Santa Goes Postal

Bob McLean, a letter carrier from Bellevue, Washington, has spent the last decade dressing as Santa Claus while delivering the mail. He even grows out his white beard to make the look more authentic. And while it's hard to believe that anyone could have a problem with Santa, apparently not everyone who works for the U.S. Postal Service is a fan.

After a coworker complained that McLean's holiday getup wasn't compliant with the U.S. Postal Service dress code, his supervisor told him he had to stop wearing the Santa outfit. But McLean was having none of it: he continued to wear the suit, insisting that people along his route loved it. "I'm kinda going rogue," McLean defiantly said. "I might get in trouble."

Fortunately, thanks to the media publicity surrounding McLean's dispute with the postal service (it even made the news in the U.K.!), his supervisor changed his mind and allowed him to keep wearing the suit.

Santa's Grammatical Family

Saint Nicholas is the main Clause.

His wife is a relative Clause.

His children are dependent Clauses.

Santa's elves are subordinate Clauses.

He Might Just Get a Speeding Ticket

Scientists have calculated that in order for Santa to deliver presents around the globe on Christmas Eve, he has to visit 822 homes a second, and travel at 650 miles per second!

Ho Ho Ho

Did you know Santa only had eight reindeer to pull his sleigh last Christmas?

That's because Comet stayed home to clean the sink!

Ho Ho Ho

A grandmother asked her grandson what he wanted for Christmas, so he showed her his lengthy list to Santa. When she commented on how long the list was, he said, "It's just in case this is the last year I believe in him!"

Santa's Helpers

A picturesque Alpine town was the scene of an unusual protest one Christmas season. Parents in the town of Antey-St-Andre in northern Italy were angered to discover that a school priest had revealed to their children that there is no Santa Claus. So the parents went to the central square in the town and asked other parents to sign a petition to remove the priest from his role at the school. The unusual part? While collecting signatures, the parents all dressed up as elves!

Parents were understandably upset that the school had revealed the Santa secret to their children. "It's not right to destroy children's dreams and it's not their place to do so," one parent said. "We're sorry that adults have forgotten the importance of this figure to children."

But the school defended the priest, who is Polish, saying that his Italian was rusty and his message was "lost in translation." This was little comfort to the parents, who remained angry elves!

When Even Santa's a Fan

Every kid eventually stops believing in Santa Claus, but child star Shirley Temple's experience was unique: "I stopped believing in Santa Claus when I was six. Mother took me to see him in a department store and he asked for my autograph."

"NOW WILL YOU BELIEVE ME?"

Christmas lights were Santa's nemesis that year.

Santa Snafu

In 2012, a Santa Claus in the U.K. suffered something of a wardrobe malfunction. The jolly man was rappelling down a rope in the middle of a shopping center during its annual Christmas lights show, when his beard became stuck in the rope. He ended up dangling 15 feet off the ground for a half hour, as another rope was lowered to rescue him.

An eyewitness to the scene said, "Everyone was laughing at him—he didn't really know what to do." Poor Santa!

Stephanie Maynard, the marketing manager at the shopping center, said the easy solution would've been for the Santa to remove his fake beard. "But he was such a professional and he didn't want to let the children down," she said. Once he was rescued, the crowd—who had stuck around after the lighting ceremony to see what would happen—cheered Santa's safe return to the earth.

Sometimes even Santa needs to call for
instructions on how to set something up.

A Delayed Santa Surprise

Construction workers renovating a home in Berkshire, England, discovered something amazing: a 70-year-old letter to Santa Claus tucked into the old chimney.

The letter, written by seven-year-old David Haylock, was written during World War II in 1944. The boy's wish list was simple: toy soldiers, chalk, a comic book, a drum, slippers, and a silk tie.

Amazingly, the workers who found the list were able to track down the nearly 80-year-old Haylock, who still lives in the area. He said he remembers receiving at least two things on his list that year: the drum and the silk tie. He said the latter was rather "precocious" to ask for. "My father probably had a silk tie and I fancied one as well," he says.

Besides reuniting Haylock with his Christmas list, the workers had one more surprise: they bought him all the gifts he requested!

These days, Santa checks his naughty and nice list digitally.

Santa's Longevity

Every savvy child knows that the Santas we see in shopping centers and parades aren't the real Santa, but rather his loyal helpers. And Raymond Lippert, of Manitowoc, Wisconsin, has been particularly loyal, donning his red Santa suit for three quarters of a century!

Lippert was only 17 years old when he first played Santa in 1941, dressing up for children at a one-room schoolhouse in the tiny Wisconsin town of Liberty. Originally reluctant to take on the role, Lippert loved the job so much that he hired a seamstress to create a custom-made suit for his next outing. Once word got around in the local community, neighbors started hiring him to deliver gifts to their homes on Christmas Eve.

Over the last 75 years, Lippert has gotten so good at transforming himself into Santa Claus that even people who know him don't always recognize him. And Lippert enjoys keeping the secret to himself!

Santa vs. the Media

A news anchor in Chicago ended up in hot water with her viewers when she announced on the air that Santa Claus isn't real. Fox anchor Robin Robinson made the gaffe during a segment about kids' Christmas gift expectations. Robinson and her cohost, Bob Sirott, started wondering what age is best to tell kids there is no Santa.

Robinson was blunt about her opinion, saying, "Stop trying to convince your kids that Santa is Santa. That's why they have these high expectations. They know you can't afford it, so what do they do? Just ask some man in a red suit. There is no Santa."

Viewers immediately complained, and Robinson apologized the next day, asking angry parents to read the famous 1897 "Yes, Virginia, There is a Santa Claus" response from the editor of the *New York Sun*.

Who would tell this happy girl that there's no Santa?

Secret Santas Down Under

In 2010, a New Zealand man came up with a modern twist on the classic Secret Santa tradition. While the gift-exchange custom is popular with office employees in the U.S., Sam Elton-Walters thought it would be fun to involve his entire country. He matched up random strangers through Twitter, and the social media users sent their partners inexpensive holiday gifts.

The idea was so popular that it was eventually taken over by the New Zealand postal service, who now take care of forwarding the Secret Santa gifts to participating Twitter users. Asking for specific gifts is discouraged—where's the fun in that? Rather, Secret Santas "lightly stalk" their assigned Twitter user for clues to their likes and dislikes, and shop accordingly.

So far, the gift exchange has been a success, with almost 2,000 Kiwis taking part in 2016. They participate at their own risk, however: New Zealand Post states that it "accepts no responsibility for inappropriateness of gifts."

Singalong Song

To the Tune of "O Little Town of Bethlehem"

O little town in the North Pole,
Home of the big red guy,
With children's presents in a heap
His trusty sleigh flies high.
And in the dark sky shineth
Rudolph's red-nosed light.
The hopes and fears of kids this year,
Are met this Christmas night.

Planes, Trains, and Sleighs

Plenty of people travel during the holidays—and of course Santa and his reindeer are the most famous travelers of all. In this chapter we'll look at planes, trains, and other modes of conveyances.

"Don't even complain about your workload
until you've pulled a sleigh in rush hour traffic."

Bet You Didn't Know

Here's a surprising fact: the crew that pulls Santa's sleigh—Dasher, Dancer, Prancer, Vixen, Comet, Cupid, Donner, Blitzen, and of course, Rudolph—are all female!

Think about the pictures you've seen depicting Santa's sleigh and his loyal reindeer: the reindeer always have antlers, right? Well, male reindeer actually shed their antlers after the mating season at the beginning of December. Whereas female reindeer have antlers throughout the entire winter. So if those pictures of Santa's reindeer are accurate, the jolly old man has a very feminist employment policy!

What's more, it makes perfect sense for the Christmas helpers to be female. Male reindeer carry only around 5 percent body fat during the holiday season, but females have about 50 percent. The extra fat keeps them nice and warm throughout the winter, making them the perfect companions at the chilly North Pole.

The reindeer weren't Santa's first attempt at this flying thing.

Santa got great speed the year he used the helicopter, but parents complained about the noise.

After that year, Santa never left the keys in the ignition again.

A Jewel of a Marketing Idea

Would you buy jewelry made of reindeer dung? What if it was marketed as "Magical Reindeer Gems"? A zoo in Illinois did just that, and the result was surprisingly popular!

The Miller Park Zoo in Bloomington began their foray into reindeer-dung recycling by creating dime-sized dung ornaments. Zoo patrons went wild for the ornaments, and requested jewelry made of the unconventional medium. The zoo obliged, adding necklaces to their deer-dung inventory.

The droppings, which come from actual reindeer at the zoo, are dehydrated, sterilized, and painted with glitter. Since their creation in 2008, the "gem" ornaments and necklaces have raised more than $50,000 for the Miller Park Zoological Society.

Requests for the unusual trinkets have even come in from all over the world; but federal regulations prohibit the export of reindeer dung, no matter what kind of "magical" name it goes by!

It would appear that Beagles were a poor choice for a sled team....

A Seat for Thee, a Seat for Your Tree

Are you travelling this Christmas? Does the idea of searching for a perfect tree at your destination sound like too much trouble? Well, if you happen to be flying Austria's Fly Niki airline, you're in luck: you can bring your own tree with you!

The airline allows passengers to fly with their Christmas trees to any of their international destinations. Even better? It's free! The only restrictions? The tree can be no more than six and a half feet tall, and you have to book your tree at least 48 hours in advance. But maybe it's worth it to know your holiday destination will be decked out just the way you like it!

Hundreds of people have already taken advantage of the offer, and the airline expects the policy will continue to be popular. Niki is known for being holiday-friendly: they play Christmas music on their planes throughout the season, and even offer punch and traditional Glühwein on flights after 6 p.m.

Ho Ho Ho

A boy was shopping with his father on Christmas Eve, when they saw a train set in a department store. "I'll take it," the father proclaimed to a salesgirl.

The girl smiled and said, "I'm sure your son will love it."

The father looked thoughtful, then replied, "Maybe you're right. In that case, I'll take two!"

Christmas Train Trivia

When you think of Christmas transportation, chances are trains are at the top of the nostalgia list. And plenty of railways across the country are now providing kids (and adults!) special excursions and attractions full of holiday magic!

Fifty different locations across the country, including Chicago and New Orleans, offer the *Polar Express* Train Ride. Based on the book of the same name, the trains provide hot chocolate and feature a visit from Santa.

On the Elf Limited, in Cass, West Virginia, passengers are treated to a theatrical performance about Santa's elf-training camp during an hour-long journey through pine forests.

And at Union Station in St. Louis, train passengers can watch ice skating and a light show before boarding Santa's Express to visit Santa's house and toy factory, and are treated to a reading of "A Visit from St. Nicholas." So all aboard for some traveling Christmas fun!

Ho Ho Ho

When is a boat like a pile of snow?

When it's adrift!

Ho Ho Ho

How do snowmen get around?

On their icicles!

Ho Ho Ho

What's the difference between Santa's reindeer and a medieval knight?

One slays the dragon, and the other is draggin' the sleigh!

Ho Ho Ho

A Viking named Rudolph the Red was gazing out his window and proclaimed that it would rain the next day.

"How do you know?" his wife asked.

He replied, "Because Rudolph the Red knows rain, dear."

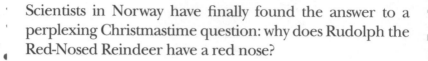

The Famous Red Nose

Scientists in Norway have finally found the answer to a perplexing Christmastime question: why does Rudolph the Red-Nosed Reindeer have a red nose?

In a not-entirely-serious study, scientists used a hand-held microscope to look at the nasal passages of humans and compare them to the noses of reindeer. They discovered that reindeer have 25 percent more blood vessels surrounding their noses than humans have. The blood vessels help to control the reindeer's body temperature, which is especially important when you have to fly around the world on a cold December night.

The results of the study were published in the *British Medical Journal*'s Christmas edition, where researchers observed, "Rudolph's nose is red because it is richly supplied with red blood cells, comprises a highly dense microcirculation, and is anatomically and physiologically adapted for reindeer to carry out their flying duties for Santa Claus."

As he tugged, Rudolph reflected that he really needed to ask for a bigger Christmas bonus.

Reindeer Crossing

Border control has been a hotly contested topic lately, but there's one group that never needs to worry about traveling in or out of the country: Santa's reindeer.

Every year, the U.S. Department of Agriculture issues a permit to allow the reindeer to legally entire the U.S. They describe the reindeer border-crossing requirements on their website at www.usda.gov, just before the Christmas season.

Santa's helpers are allowed to cross into the U.S. between 6 p.m. on December 24 and 6 a.m. on December 25. To speed the process along, they waive requirements that the animals be tested for diseases, even allowing one reindeer with "Rednose Syndrome" to enter the country. But the reindeer must never have eaten anything other than hay, sugar plums, and gingerbread, and they must all respond to their given names.

Who knew the USDA had such a great sense of humor?

Santa's no stranger to bureaucracy! This 1927 picture
shows Santa Claus receiving an "aeroplane pilot's license"
from the Assistant Secretary of Commerce.

Did Dasher and Dancer Decide on a Diet?

It's no secret that Santa could stand to lose a few pounds. But it's actually his reindeer who are getting smaller! Scottish scientists studied reindeer in Norway between 1994 and 2015, and discovered that their average weight shrank from 121 pounds to 106 pounds.

The Norwegian reindeer, who live about 800 miles from the North Pole, use their antlers to dig through snow and find plants to eat in the winter. But recent winter rainfalls have resulted in blankets of ice that make reaching the plants more difficult. To compound the problem, warmer summers have created an abundance of plant life, which has led to an abundance of reindeer! More reindeer, searching for less-accessible food, means a smaller Rudolph for Santa's sleigh.

Then again, perhaps all that sleigh-pulling exercise has created more svelte reindeer. Santa should take note!

Ho Ho Ho

A news station excitedly reported a sighting of an unidentified flying object on Christmas Eve. The news reporter described it, of course, as a U-F-ho-ho-ho.

Singalong Song

To the Tune of "Away in a Manger"

We're stuck in the airport, so far from our beds,
On chairs of cold plastic we lay down our heads.
The words on the bright screen tell us of delays,
While outside the airplanes are stuck on runways.
Oh Christmas is coming, but we are delayed,
We sigh and we wish that at home we had stayed.
We watch snow and sleet as they fall from the sky,
And hope that a patch of good weather is nigh.

Have Yourself a Historical Little Christmas

A shocking scandal: This 1860s image shows that in his more youthful days, Santa was a smoker! Who could have guessed?

A Different Kind of Christmas Card

Back in World War II, the Red Cross distributed Christmas parcels to POWs in Europe. The Nazis who guarded the prisoners allowed the packages to be handed out, never suspecting that anything within the innocent-looking items could be amiss. But one item given to the POWs—a deck of playing cards—was more than it appeared.

Bicycle brand playing cards teamed up with American and British intelligence agencies to create maps with escape routes for the POWs. Of course the maps had to be hidden, so the playing card company created special cards that peeled apart when they got wet, revealing the maps. Because playing cards were such a common item amongst the prisoners, the Nazis were none the wiser!

The clever cards helped at least 32 people escape Nazi camps and find their way back to Allied territory. Now that's a great Christmas gift!

Ho, Ho...Boo?

If you know the words to the classic holiday song "It's the Most Wonderful Time of the Year," you may have wondered about some of the lyrics. The song describes holiday festivities to come, like parties and caroling, but also says that "there'll be scary ghost stories." Did the songwriters confuse Christmas with Halloween?

Well, it turns out that telling ghost stories at Christmas used to be an English tradition in Victorian times. In fact, is was such a ubiquitous part of a Victorian Christmas that British humorist Jerome K. Jerome wrote in 1891, "Whenever five or six English-speaking people meet round a fire on Christmas Eve, they start telling each other ghost stories. Nothing satisfies us on Christmas Eve but to hear each other tell authentic anecdotes about specters."

While the ghost-story tradition has mostly died out, it does remain a part of our modern Christmas—even in America—in the form of yearly readings and performances of Charles Dickens' classic *A Christmas Carol.*

Did You Know?

It only took Charles Dickens one month to write his classic tale *A Christmas Carol,* which he wrote between October and November 1843. The story was an immediate hit, selling 6,000 copies by Christmas Day.

Just Say No

Did you know that Christmas was once banned in Boston? The holiday was deemed unacceptable by Puritans in the Massachusetts Bay Colony from 1659 until 1681.

It wasn't necessarily the holiday itself that bristled the Puritan's bonnets; rather, it was the celebration that came along with it. The custom of "wassailing" was popular at the time, when lower-class citizens would demand food and wine from wealthier neighbors, and refusals would often turn violent.

But the Puritan law also banned holiday delicacies like mince pies and puddings. Even wishing someone "Merry Christmas" would result in a five-shilling fine. And colonists were required to work on Christmas Day. Even after the holiday was reinstated in 1681, celebrations were sparse until the late 1800s. In fact, kids who skipped school on Christmas Day often risked expulsion. Fortunately, President Ulysses S. Grant decreed the day a national holiday in 1870, and kids have looked forward to Christmas vacation ever since!

Christmas got a little too merry for the Puritans.

A Little Bit Dangerous

Glittering streams of tinsel are a Christmastime tradition. The shiny decoration derives its name from the Old French word *estincele*, which means "sparkle," and may have originally been used on Christmas trees in Germany to reflect candlelight.

But the decoration also has a secret past: it once contained dangerous amounts of lead. In 1972, the FDA required manufacturers to change their processes to remove the lead, however, they kept the change a secret. Why? Because the lead-based tinsel was so beloved by consumers that the FDA was worried that people would stockpile the shiny stuff for later use!

Fortunately, common sense prevailed, and nowadays, tinsel is usually made of aluminum-coated plastic. The evolution of the tree adornment is a good reminder that sometimes even the shiniest traditions can benefit from a makeover.

"Look, shiny!"

Did You Know?

A reading of "A Visit from St. Nicholas"—perhaps better known by its first line, "'Twas the Night Before Christmas"— has been a holiday tradition for almost two centuries. The poem was originally published anonymously in 1823, and was later credited to Clement Clark Moore.

Legend has it Moore was reluctant to publish the poem, deeming it "beneath" his usual talent, so an unknown family member submitted it to an out-of-town newspaper. Readers immediately loved it, but it took 15 years for Clement to come forward as the author.

But did he actually write it? Don Foster, an English professor at Vassar College, suggests that Moore stole credit for the poem from writer Henry Livingston Jr., whose own writing style much more closely matches that of the poem. Livingston's family has always insisted that he was the true author.

We may never know for sure who to thank for "A Visit from St. Nicholas," but it will undoubtedly will continue to be a part of our holiday traditions!

'Twas the night before Christmas, and this little girl was determined to hang up her stocking!

Christmas Around the World

Some Christmas traditions are sweet, some strange. We'll take a look at customs from around the world.

Even Santa is sometimes surprised by how people celebrate Christmas.

How High?

A giant snowman named Snowzilla has been built every year since 2005 in front of Alaskan Billy Powers' home in Anchorage. The huge snowman has ranged from 16 feet to 25 feet high!

This snowman might be Snowzilla's cousin.

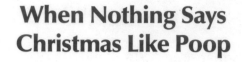

When Nothing Says
Christmas Like Poop

One of the world's most unusual holiday traditions has to be Tio de Nadal, or Christmas Log, from the Catalonia region of Spain. Every year, families choose a hollowed-out log, paint it with a cute face, prop it up, and cover it with blankets (to keep it warm, of course). Beginning on December 8, the anthropomorphic log is "fed" candies, nuts, and treats every night.

But the truly bizarre part comes on Christmas Day, when the log—which is popularly known as "Caga Tio," or "pooping log"—is placed in the fireplace and beaten with sticks. As the holiday celebrants hit the log, they sing songs to encourage it to "poop" all the candies and treats. And with lyrics like, "if you don't poop well; I'll hit you with a stick," how could it not comply?

Although the Christmas Log tradition has been around for centuries, the "poop log" expression is, unsurprisingly, a much newer addition to the festivities!

It Really Gets Your Goat

In Scandinavia, it is traditional to see goats—known as Yule goats—depicted in ornaments and on holiday cards. But the town of Gavle, Sweden, takes the tradition to new heights. Every year since 1966, the town has constructed a giant, 43-foot tall, three-ton goat made of straw, which is placed in Castle Square.

The festive goat is supposed to remain in the square from the beginning of Advent until a few days after the New Year. But the giant collection of straw has proven to be far too appealing to vandals. Since its original appearance, the poor goat has been burned down 36 times.

Ironically, the town's fire department is located close to the square. In fact, the first Gavle goat was constructed by members of the fire department. It was then burned down by vandals on New Year's Eve.

Perhaps the burning of the Gavle goat is now as much a tradition as its display!

Real estate had been cheap at the North Pole, but Santa
wished he'd been able to make his base in the tropics.

Christmas on the Beach

If your idea of a perfect Christmas is sunshine, warm weather, and beaches, you're not alone. According to a survey conducted by the ALDI grocery store chain of shoppers in America, the U.K., and Australia, the Land Down Under is considered the most desirable Christmas Day destination.

The survey found that people appreciate the warm weather and the opportunity to spend the holiday outdoors. Those surveyed also cited less time in the kitchen as a selling point. Australians usually spend about two hours cooking the holiday meal, whereas Americans and Brits are stuck in the kitchen for four hours or more. The novelty of the Australian Christmas dinner menu, which tends to include plenty of seafood, fresh fruit, and salads, is appealing for those visitors who are looking to change up their usual traditions.

And Christmas Day on the beach would certainly be a break in tradition for many of us!

Rolling On Down

Does driving or walking to a Christmas church service seem too boring? Then perhaps you should head down to Caracas, Venezuela. The city has a fun and unique tradition when it comes to holiday transportation: the entire city roller skates to Christmas mass!

The city has early-morning mass services every day from December 16 to December 24, and the streets are closed to cars until 8 a.m. to allow the crowds of roller skaters to pass. Children in the city have an unusual custom, as well: each night, they tie a long piece of string around their big toe, and allow the other end to dangle out the window. In the morning, roller skaters give the strings playful tugs as they pass by!

After attending the church services, families head out to enjoy tostados and coffee. And after burning all those calories skating, they deserve it!

Santa tried it out, but decided to stick with his
reindeer in the long term.

When It's Time to Toss the Tree

If you're like most people, when Christmas is over you drag your tree out to the curb or throw it in a trash bin, and then let someone else figure out what to do with it. But if you lived in Weidenthal, Germany, the end of the Christmas season would signal the beginning of the Annual Christmas Tree Throwing World Championship!

The strange festival is held each year on January 5, where hundreds of participants gather in the south-German town to show off their tree-flinging skills. There are competitions in "javelin-style"—where competitors throw their trees like javelins, as far as they can—"hammer-style"—where the tree is swung around in a circle before being released—and "high jump-style"—where competitors hurl their trees over a high-jump bar.

Whoever throws their tree the farthest total distance is the winner—although it's unclear whether the "winner" of this competition receives anything other than tree-tossing bragging rights!

Christmas at the Other Pole

You would think that spending Christmas in Antarctica would be cold, lonely, and perhaps a bit boring. But the scientists and workers who live there during the holidays have given the continent its own traditions for the season.

Since Antarctica is in the southern hemisphere, December falls in the middle of summer. So, while temperatures still tend to hover below freezing, workers can more comfortably head outside for some fun. One holiday tradition is the Christmas day "Race Around the World," where runners compete in a two-mile race that circles the South Pole, hitting every time zone in the world along the way. The winner receives a five-minute hot shower, which is a luxury compared to the two-minute showers normally allowed!

To ring in the New Year, workers at the South Pole Station hold a ceremony to readjust the pole. The Antarctic ice sheet drifts about 30 feet every year, requiring a "new" South Pole for the new year.

What to Do in Snowless Climes

Those of us who live in America have many deep-seated ideas about what constitutes a traditional Christmas. Falling snow, holly boughs, roasted turkeys, piping hot pumpkin pies—all of the cold-weather images we've known since childhood. But what about people who celebrate the holiday in warmer climates?

In South Africa, people often go camping for the holiday, and eat Christmas dinner outdoors. Australians love to decorate with wreaths and lights, and spend the day swimming. It's so warm that most Aussies enjoy cold Christmas dinners, or they have a barbecue with prawns, lobster, or other seafood. In Kenya, Christmas trees are often Cyprus trees, and houses are decorated with balloons, ribbons, flowers, and leaves. In Sri Lanka, Christians celebrate the beginning of the holiday season on December 1 with fire crackers, and Christians and non-Christians all gather together for Christmas parties.

It's clear to see that snow is not a necessity for a very Merry Christmas!

Missing: Frosty. Last seen heading south for the winter.

A Finger Lickin' Christmas

Onc of the things everyone looks forward to around the holidays is the food. Christmas turkeys, Christmas hams, Christmas cookies, Christmas… KFC? Yes, if you lived in Japan, chances are you'd be ordering your holiday meal from the fried chicken restaurant. In fact, KFC on Christmas has become such a Japanese tradition that families order weeks in advance to make sure they'll have their Kentucky Fried Christmas dinner!

The unusual trend began back in 1970, when the first KFC opened in Japan. Takeshi Okawara, the manager of the store, heard some foreigners talking about how they missed turkey dinners on Christmas. So Okawara came up with the idea to offer a "party barrel" of chicken for the holiday.

Since Japan has no real Christmas traditions, the idea was an immediate hit with Japanese families. Nowadays, the "party barrel" also comes with cake and wine, and families can even order an entire whole chicken. It almost sounds good enough to forgo the turkey!

The Christmas Pickle

You may have heard of the famous German holiday tradition of the *Weihnachtsgurke*, or Christmas Pickle. As the story goes, on Christmas Eve, the last ornament placed on the tree is a pickle-shaped ornament, which is hidden amongst the green branches. The first child to find the ornament on Christmas morning is said to have good luck in the coming year, and is given an extra gift.

It seems like a nice tradition, but there's one problem: very few people in Germany—where the custom supposedly originated—have actually heard of it! In fact, in a 2016 survey of 2,057 Germans, 91 percent of the respondents had never heard of the Christmas Pickle.

Surprisingly, the more likely origin for the "German" tradition of the Christmas Pickle is the United States, where the town of Berrien Springs, Michigan is known as the "Christmas Pickle capital of the world"!

Did You Know?

Bookworms should head to Iceland for the Christmas season: it's tradition to exchange books on Christmas Eve, and read for the rest of the night. New books in the small country are generally only published towards the end of the year, creating the book-buying frenzy.

Just Say No...to Christmas?

The Grinch has taken his attitude to China! A Chinese university banned Christmas from its campus, calling it a "'kitsch' foreign celebration." Instead, students are forced to watch propaganda films and learn about Confucius.

One student said that screening the films was mandatory, and professors were standing guard to prevent anyone from leaving. "There's nothing we can do about it, we can't escape," the student said.

China is officially atheist, but Christmas is becoming more popular in the country, especially among young people in populated metropolitan areas, who also love U.S. pop culture. But the ruling Communist Party sees it as an "obsession" with the West, and prefers that young people focus on their own Chinese heritage, customs, and holidays.

The ironic part? Many of the artificial trees and Christmas decorations we use in the United States are made in China!

The Yule Lads

Ask any American child who brings their presents at Christmastime, and they'll tell you it's Santa Claus. But Icelandic children don't have a simple answer: they have 13 different Santas!

They're called the "Yule Lads," and the gnome-like creatures all take turns visiting kids on the 13 nights leading up to Christmas. Children put their shoes on the windowsill at night, and in the morning (if they've been good) they are filled with candy. Naughty children are given rotten potatoes!

Each Yule Lad has a different personality, and is known for playing pranks. There's "Stubby," who likes to steal food from frying pans; "Pot Scraper," who takes unwashed pots and licks them clean; and "Door Slammer," who keeps everyone in the house awake with his raucous noise—just to name a few.

The Yule Lads used to be a much scarier bunch, but in 1746, parents were banned from telling their kids unsettling stories about them!

A Novel Idea

The twinkling lights, cheerful songs, and colorful packages are all part of what makes the month of December so magical. But what if that magic was postponed until February?

Slate editor L.V. Anderson suggests we should do just that. In an article she wrote for the online publication, Anderson argues that December 25 falls too close to Thanksgiving, which doesn't give us enough time to recover from one huge holiday meal before partaking of another. The writer also points out that part of what makes Christmas such a beloved time of year is the happiness and cheer it brings to a cold winter month. But after the holiday, we are left with three more months of bleak winter weather. If Christmas fell in the middle of February, all of that holiday cheer could help warm us up during the dark months of midwinter.

So how about it? Should we deck the halls in February instead of December?

Christmastime Crime

Some pretty weird crimes have popped up during the holiday season. In this chapter we'll share some of them.

North Pole
Police Dept.

Claus, Santa
12/24/2010

The reindeer tried to say he was just in the area and had never met the others before, but the police didn't buy it.

Stuck!

There are some ways that we mere mortals should never try to be like Santa Claus. Take climbing down chimneys, for instance. Santa has Christmas magic on his side. But Seattle man Shon Shanell thought he could slide down a chimney just as easily as the jolly old man. Not surprisingly, he was wrong!

Police say that Shanell was planning to rob a house by breaking in through the chimney. Unfortunately for the would-be burglar, he got stuck and had to yell for help. Firefighters spent almost an hour chiseling away bricks to reach the man, who, inexplicably, turned out to be naked. Perhaps he thought his bulky clothing would impede his descent through the tight space, but it ended up being all for naught!

Shanell, who was dubbed the "Santa Claus burglar," claimed he was only trying to retrieve a backpack which had been tossed down the chimney. But a judge and jury didn't buy the story, and he was sentenced to 17 months in prison.

Ho Ho Ho No

A Christmas Eve tweet from the York Regional Police in Aurora, Ontario, reminded "Citizens may hear hoof steps on your roofs tonight and should not be alarmed. If anyone other than Santa comes down your chimney, call us!"

Kris Kingle is the only man you want to see in your chimney.

A Step beyond Savvy Shopping

Many people would go to great lengths to give the kids in their lives a happy Christmas. But a couple of thieves in Polk County, Florida, went too far in 2014.

Tarus Scott and Gerard Dupree were shopping at a Walmart, where Scott filled a cart with a Barbie car, a Leap Frog tablet, and a Barbie vacation house. As the pair neared the exit, Dupree dramatically clutched his chest and fell to the ground, faking a heart attack. As customers and security guards rushed to his aid, Scott was able to push the cart out the door, unnoticed by the crowd gathered around his friend.

Once Scott was outside, Dupree made a "miraculous" recovery and walked away, rejoining his friend in the parking lot.

Of course, in this day and age, someone is always watching: the entire caper was caught on surveillance video, and the two were quickly arrested.

Fluffy had promised to go straight, but faced with temptation, he caved.

Stick 'em Up Santa

Santa Claus is supposed to be a symbol of peace and joy. So when someone dressed like Santa robs a bank, it's even more startling than a regular bank heist!

Just before Christmas in 2016, a man dressed in a Santa mask walked into a bank in Memphis, Tennessee, and handed a teller a note demanding money. After the teller turned over some money, the robber fled on foot (not by sleigh!).

But that's not the strangest part of the story. Before robbing the bank, the man had been passing out candy and wishing everyone in the bank Merry Christmas. Surveillance video posted on the Memphis Police Department's Facebook page shows the Kris-Kringle-masked man calmly walking through the bank, offering tellers and customers candy canes. He then walks back to one of the tellers and gives her his demand note.

At least the robber spread some holiday cheer before breaking the law!

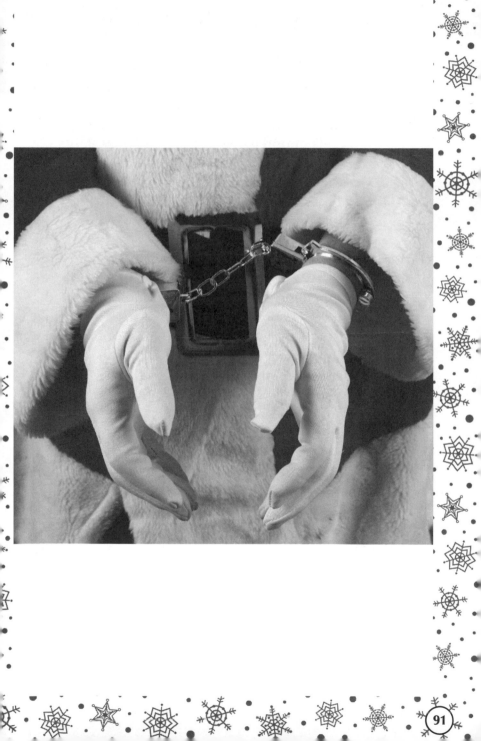

An Illuminating Crime

The Montrose Shopping Park in Glendale, California, dealt with a string of unusual thefts during the 2016 Christmas season. Instead of taking merchandise or breaking into any stores, the thieves were making off with thousands of dollars' worth of Christmas lights!

The lights were taken from the trees that line both sides of Honolulu Avenue, the main thoroughfare through the shopping center.

Dale Dawson, the business administrator for the shopping center, says this is the first time anything like this has happened, and he suspects that some of the thefts occurred in broad daylight, because lights that were on trees in the afternoon were gone by evening. "It's a head-scratcher that someone could be so bold," he said. Dawson thinks the thieves may have sold the stolen lights.

Even though the stolen lights added up to more than $2,000, the shopping center replaced all of them, wanting to continue to provide a festive holiday location for shoppers.

Ho Ho Ho

At Christmastime, a judge asked a defendant, "What are you charged with?"

The defendant replied, "Doing my Christmas shopping a little early."

Confused, the judge said, "That's not a crime. How early were you doing your shopping?"

The defendant replied, "Before the store opened."

Some Strange Christmas Ornaments

Residents of Naples, Italy, were dismayed one Christmas season to discover that a 20-foot tall tree in the Galleria Umberto had been stolen. It's bad enough for thieves to steal a Christmas tree, but the tree in the famous shopping center is known for being a "wishing tree": people write their wishes on slips of paper and attach them to the tree. A similar tradition surrounds religious monuments in the city, which are sometimes found to contain scraps of paper with wishes scrawled on them.

So to combat the threat of holiday hijinks, the city came up with a solution: padlocks and chains! Perhaps the unusual adornments aren't as awe-inspiring as many of the traditional festive decorations we're used to, but for practical purposes, they get the job done.

And the "wishing tree" isn't the only locked up tree: trees all across the city have been chained to staircases and railings to prevent pilfering. Whatever works!

Ho Ho Ho

An honest politician, a generous lawyer, and Santa Claus were riding a hotel elevator. They noticed a $100 bill on the floor, but only one of them turned it in to the front desk.

Which one?

Santa Claus, of course—the other two don't exist!

A Weed-y Good Present

A man thought he was being clever when he found a unique way to transport thousands of dollars' worth of marijuana across state lines: he wrapped the drugs like Christmas presents!

Unfortunately for Daniel A. Yates, of Eureka, California, he was stopped by state troopers on Interstate 80 in Ohio for following the car in front of him too closely. The troopers thought that Yates was acting suspicious, and a drug-sniffing dog alerted them to something in Yates' rented Ford Expedition. In the back, the troopers discovered 10 gift-wrapped boxes, which were found to contain 71 pounds of marijuana, 360 THC pills, and a pound of hash wax oil.

Needless to say, Yates did not have a merry Christmas—he was incarcerated in an Ohio county jail and charged with possession and drug trafficking. A conviction could mean 16 holidays in prison for the crafty Christmas criminal.

The Cannabis Christmas tree that cousin Jake set up was a big hit with Grandpa and Grandma.

Drunk, Disorderly...and Mean!

It's rare to see a holiday Grinch get his comeuppance. But spectators at a Kingston, Ontario, Christmas parade got the satisfaction of watching just that. A 24-year-old drunk man was walking next to the parade route. But his public intoxication wasn't the worst part: the Christmas-magic crusher was telling children along the parade route that Santa Claus doesn't exist!

Fortunately, officers from the Kingston Police Department found the inebriated man and arrested him. Reportedly, he was easy to find because of his disturbing hairstyle—his hair was "formed to look like horns that were protruding from his head." Sounds like someone could've used a big dose of (non-alcoholic) Christmas spirit! The parade interloper was charged with causing a disturbance by being drunk and breach of probation.

Kidnapped!

A little girl in Australia was heartbroken when her favorite decorations, a pair of light-up reindeer, were stolen from her yard one evening in December 2016. The girl, nine-year-old Chiara Velardi, was interviewed on the news after the incident, which resulted in something unexpected: an apology from the thief.

The robber wrote Velardi a note by hand, which began, "To whoever's Christmas I destroyed. I'm very sorry for taking your Raindeer. I was unaware of my actions due to being drunk." Despite not knowing how to spell "reindeer," the thief seemed to be genuine in his remorse, adding, "I hope this letter makes you feel better. I'm so sorry once again I promise to never do this again. Please feel safe and have a nice Christmas!" He also enclosed $100, so Velardi could buy new decorations.

In the spirit of the Christmas season, the little girl forgave the robber. And next year, maybe he'll try a little harder to avoid Santa's "naughty" list!

Giving "Christmas Break" a New Meaning

If you were in prison, your idea of a Christmas miracle would probably be the perfect opportunity for a prison break. For six inmates in the Cocke County jail in Newport, Tennessee, their holiday wishes came true on Christmas Day. The group broke out of the prison after they removed an old toilet from the wall and crawled out through the hole behind it.

The inmates benefitted from an old plumbing system with a history of repairs, weak spots, and rust, which made tunneling through the concrete wall easier. They also, it would seem, had nothing better to do. "It's the product of them having nothing to do 24 hours a day for seven days a week except think of how to tear things up," said Cocke County Sherriff Armando Fontes.

Their freedom was short-lived, however. All six of the escapees were back in prison three days later, just in time for the New Year.

A Costly Treat

Panettone cakes are a popular Christmas dessert in parts of Europe and Latin America. The cakes are full of candied fruits and raisins, and enjoyed throughout the holiday season.

So when Italian police found one of the Christmas confections in the trunk of a businessman's car in the middle of spring, they were suspicious. And rightfully so: instead of finding a cake filled with candied fruits, they discovered it was filled with money—250,000 to be exact! The 47-year-old businessman turned out to be a money launderer and tax evader, who also had 1.2 million stashed away in his basement, under a trapdoor hidden by the washing machine. He owed 300,000 in taxes.

Perhaps next time, he'll use some of his secret cash stash to buy a more seasonally appropriate pastry in which to hide his money!

A New Use for a Christmas Tree

It's not unusual for family arguments to break out around holiday time; but it is unusual to use the Christmas tree as a weapon. But that's what one woman in York County, Pennsylvania did during a family scuffle.

Karen Harrelson was at her grandmother's house when another guest in the house, Kayla Still, asked her not to light a cigarette in the home. Harrelson argued with Still, verbally threatening her, and the fight escalated until Harrelson picked up her grandmother's Christmas tree and hurled it at Still. Police were called, and Harrelson was charged with assault.

This wasn't Harrelson's first offense: in 2013 she was arrested for stabbing Gregory Stambaugh when they argued over who should win *American Idol*. But it's likely that she'll now be remembered as the woman who wielded a Christmas tree as a weapon!

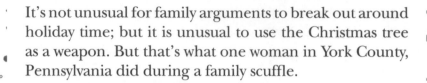

Eat, Drink, and Be Merry

Gingerbread cookies. Mulled wine. Candy canes. In this chapter we'll look at the foods and drinks of Christmas. Fair warning: You may end up hungry.

Stuck in the chimney, Santa had ample time to reflect on his Christmas cookie habit.

Peppermint as Edible Pacifier?

Peppermint: love it or hate it, the flavor is everywhere during the holiday season. It flavors seasonal coffees, cookies, teas, cakes, and of course, candy canes. So how did the frosty flavor become synonymous with Christmas?

The candy cane itself might be the answer. One story says that in 1670, a choirmaster in Germany was looking for a way to keep boisterous children quiet during Christmas church services. So he asked a confectioner to create a special hard candy shaped like a shepherd's staff. The shape of the candy reflected back to the shepherds in the nativity story, which the kids could quietly sit through as they happily ate their sweets.

Unfortunately, there's no real evidence that the candy-cane origin story is true. But true or not, peppermint has taken hold as the flavor of the season, and we'll no doubt be drinking peppermint mochas for many Christmases to come!

The snowman didn't care what the drink
was, as long as it was cold.

all you need
is love
and
Christmas
cookies

#WhopperExchange

We've all been recipients of disappointing gifts on Christmas morning. But what's an ungrateful gift beneficiary to do? Well, Burger King has a solution: exchange those less-than-ideal presents for delicious burgers!

In 2016, the fast food giant featured a "Whopper Exchange" on December 26. Customers in select locations in Miami, London, and Brazil could bring in a present that failed to meet their expectations, and hand it over in exchange for a free Whopper. The gifts had to be unused, and whether they were acceptable for the exchange was "determined by Burger King Restaurant personnel in their sole discretion."

And Burger King patrons in other cities could participate, as well. The first 100 people to post a picture of their undesirable gift with the hashtag #WhopperExchange received "a surprise from the Burger King brand's social media accounts."

All of the gifts collected went to charity, so those unwanted gifts didn't go to waste!

Speaking of Burger King

Restaurants frequently feature special menu items for the holiday season, and Burger King in Israel is no exception. The fast food establishment created a special Whopper just for Hanukkah called the "SufganiKing."

In case you're wondering, the name is derived from "sufganiyah," which is the Hebrew word for doughnut. And yes, the burger—which comes with the usual beef patty, lettuce, ketchup, mayonnaise, pickles, and onions— is served between two doughnuts instead of buns!

During the Hanukkah season, doughnuts in Israel are usually filled with jelly. But, in another match-up of sweet and savory, the doughnuts in the SufganiKing burger are filled with ketchup.

Steve Ben Shimol, the CEO of Burger King Israel, said that combining the two popular foods was "inevitable." He added, "We're proud to be able to end 2016 on a creative, festive note."

CHRISTMAS CALORIES DON'T COUNT

Ho Ho Ho

People are so worried about what they eat between Christmas and the New Year, but they really should be worried about what they eat between the New Year and Christmas!

Christmas Year Round

Are you one of those people who says they could eat Christmas dinner every single day? Well, Jayne Winteringham of Bristol, England, actually does eat a Christmas feast every day. What's more, she swears that her unusual diet helps to keep her weight steady.

Winteringham started her tradition when her four children left home. She found it easy to just roast some meat and vegetables for her dinner, and it soon became a habit. You would think that the same meal day in and day out would get boring, but Winteringham says she never gets tired of it. "It's what I like to eat when I get home from work," she insists.

And the consistency has helped her stay in shape. "I never put weight on. I'm the same size as I was when I was 18," she says. "I always have the same calories—I don't fluctuate."

Bring on the turkey and gravy!

One Way to Have a Merry Christmas

Is trying to follow a healthy diet during the holidays stressing you out? Actress and singer Bette Midler tweeted a possible solution: "Happy holidays to all: Here is my recipe for dairy-free, sugar-free, vegan eggnog: Bourbon."

Santa really liked the houses where they
left him a martini.

If You're Really Desperate for a Midnight Snack

Did you know that Christmas trees are edible? Many parts of pine, spruce, and fir trees can be eaten, and the needles are a good source of vitamin C. And pine nuts, which come from pine cones, are already popular for making pesto and even cookies!

Maybe this chipmunk has squirreled away
some pine needles for later?

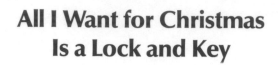

All I Want for Christmas Is a Lock and Key

If you're craving an omelet at 3 a.m., there's always one place you can count on to be open: Denny's. The diner, which started franchising in 1963, has always been known for its 24-hour, 7-days-a-week model, even remaining open on holidays.

But in 1988, Denny's management decided to do something it had never done before: close on Christmas to give all its employees the day off.

It was a nice gesture, but there was one problem. Since none of the restaurants had ever closed before, many of them were built without locks. And even though some of the diners had locks, many of the keys (which had never been used) had been lost!

So management was forced to add locks to many restaurants, and make new keys for the restaurants with locks—all for one single day of the year.

The really funny part? Denny's decided to never close on Christmas again!

Yum, Christmas Fish

If you live in America, chances are you've had a traditional Christmas dinner of turkey with all the trimmings at least once or twice. You may have even heard of Germany's love of Christmas goose. But some very interesting holiday meal traditions are found all around the world.

In the Philippines, holiday gatherings call for a whole roasted pig, stuffed with onions, lemongrass, and garlic. In Poland, no holiday is complete without Christmas *pierogi*—dumplings filled with mashed potatoes, cottage cheese, or sauerkraut. Latin Americans enjoy tamales at Christmastime, with each country putting its own spin on the ingredients used.

But perhaps the most unusual food tradition comes from Russia, where holiday meals include a salad with the colorful name "herring in a fur coat." The dish includes layers of beets, potatoes, hard boiled eggs, mayo, and, of course, herring!

Gingerbread for the Masses!

Gingerbread houses are a fun—and delicious—staple during the holiday season. But gingerbread, and the intricately decorated confections made from it, wasn't always available to the common masses.

Ginger was first introduced to Europe in 992 by an Armenian monk named Gregory of Nicopolis. The spice was originally used for religious purposes: bakers would add it to bread dough and knead it into a moldable paste, which was then carved into religious figures and painted with icing.

Gingerbread was also thought to ease indigestion and have medicinal properties. But it was so prized by European royalty that a "gingerbread guild" controlled the production of the product.

But after the Brothers Grimm published their famous story "Hansel and Gretel," about two children who discover an evil witch's edible candy house in a forest, the creation of gingerbread houses became immensely popular, and a Christmas tradition was born!

"Look, if this Santa guy doesn't come until after midnight, what do you expect from us?"

Singalong Song

To the Tune of "Joy to the World"

Joy to the world,
The roast is done.
Let us sit down and eat,
But everyone make sure to leave some room,
For cookies and sweet treats,
For cookies and sweet treats,
For cookies, oh cookies,
and sweet treats.

O Christmas Tree

For many people, the decorations are key to enjoying the holiday—especially the Christmas tree. We'll look at trees and other decorations in this chapter, from the beautiful to the bizarre.

Go Ugly or Go Home

Plenty of cities have been home to what their residents call "ugly" Christmas trees. But in 2016, the tree in the center of the Piazza Venezia in Rome, Italy, was dubbed "the ugliest in the world."

The mayor of Rome, Virginia Raggi, held a tree-lighting ceremony to light the 65-foot tall tree in early December. But when the tree was illuminated, instead of the customary oohs and ahs that usually accompany such events, the crowd reacted with total silence. The sparse fir appeared to be haphazardly draped in a sad few strings of lights, with no other decorations.

Posts under the tree's picture on Facebook were not kind, with residents saying "Even in war-torn Iraq they have a better tree!" and "It's just like the rest of the city—full of holes and covered in rubbish." Ouch!

Let's hope Rome's next Christmas tree will be one befitting of the Eternal City!

NEVER WORRY ABOUT THE SIZE OF YOUR CHRISTMAS TREE. IN THE EYES OF CHILDREN, THEY ARE ALL 30 FEET TALL.

Didn't It Clash with the Pumpkins?

How early is too early to put up Christmas decorations? A bit before Thanksgiving? Halloween? How about two weeks before Halloween?

That's when the Citadel Outlets mall, a shopping center near downtown Los Angeles, put up their holiday decorations in 2016.

The mall is known for its self-proclaimed "world's biggest bow"—a gigantic sparkly red bow that adorns the roof of the shopping center—but motorists noticed that it was displayed much earlier than usual.

The mall's spokesperson, Chelsea Hartnett, admitted that "it seems early" to have to bow out in October, but insisted that it was keeping with the Citadel's decoration schedule. The mall's adornment also includes a giant reindeer, oversized ornaments, and a 115-foot live tree.

With stores around the country seemingly decorating earlier and earlier, it's hard not to believe that we'll one day be seeing Santa in July!

A Few Facts

You probably don't think much about the facts and figures behind your yearly Christmas tree. So here are a few to ponder:

In 2015, 26 million real trees and 13 million artificial trees were sold in the U.S. The average cost for each was $51 and $69, respectively. Since artificial trees can be used year after year, they would seem to be the better value!

It takes about seven years for a tree to grow tall enough to be used as a Christmas tree, with the most popular types being Fraser Fir, Douglas Fir, Balsam Fir, Colorado Blue Spruce, and Scotch Pine.

Green, obviously, is the most popular color for artificial trees; but trees of different colors are sold every year. White is the second-most popular color, and trees are sold in pink, purple, silver, rainbow, and even black!

And don't despair about cutting down your Christmas tree: for every tree cut, up to three seedlings are planted.

Strange but True

There was a strange hair trend popping up on social media in 2016: "Christmas tree hair." And while it may sound like hair that is simply styled with sparkly ornamentation or ribbons, it's actually quite literal.

Women were piling their hair on top of their heads in cone-like shapes, and completing the look with ornaments, bows, and tinsel. Some even colored their hair green to make them appear more tree-like.

Nadwa Yono, who owns a salon in Farmington Hills, Michigan, created one such look for a promotional photo shoot. She used a Styrofoam cone as a tree base, and then piled hair on top of it, finishing off the look with tree ornaments.

Yono says the style "can be both creative and classy," although it's hard to imagine an outing where hair shaped like a tree would seem "classy."

"No, no, this isn't heavy at all! And I love
having needles poking at my head!"

Going for Height

The city of Colombo, Sri Lanka, was proud to unveil the tallest Christmas tree in the world in 2016. The 238-foot tall artificial tree was made of steel and plastic, and covered in one million pine cones painted red, green, gold and silver. It was lit with 600,000 LED bulbs, and topped with a gleaming star that was almost 20 feet tall.

But not everyone was impressed: the Catholic Church criticized the $80,000 tree, calling it "a waste of money," and saying it would have been better to use those funds to help the poor. Prime Minister Ranil Wickremesinghe pointed out that all the money used for the tree came from private donations.

The tree was meant to be a symbol of ethnic and religious harmony in the country, which only recently saw the end of a long civil war.

Deck the Car

You probably decorate your home around the holidays, with the Christmas tree being the focal point of the holiday cheer. But what about your car? One company thinks that Christmas trees aren't just for homes, offices, or shopping centers—they also make a great centerpiece for your mode of transportation!

The website *Christmascartree.com* sells two-and-a-half-foot tall artificial Christmas trees, complete with colorful lights, to attach to the roof of your car. Each tree comes with suction cups and straps to secure it to the roof, and once it's in place, it "withstands high speeds and winter weather." The tree is collapsible, as well, in case you need to pull your decked-out car into a garage.

If you're still skeptical, consider the fact that the Christmas Car Tree was featured on a Holiday Tech segment on the *Today Show*, where Al Roker happily demonstrated the festive car topper. The tree will set you back $130, but perhaps it's worth it to show off your portable Christmas spirit!

Did You Know?

The Guinness World Record for the tallest cut Christmas tree was a 221-foot Douglas Fir displayed in the Northgate Shopping Center in Seattle, Washington, in 1950.

Just Put Down the Saw
and No One Gets Smelly

Christmas tree farms provide Americans with 25 to 30 million cut trees every year. But some people balk at the idea of paying $40 or $50 for a tree, when there are so many "free" trees available to cut down. Illegal Christmas tree poachers are a problem anywhere evergreens grow. Their perfect greenery, which would look so festive covered with lights and ornaments, is too tempting for some poachers to pass up.

So land owners have come up with some interesting deterrents to thwart would-be Christmas tree snatchers. One ingenious technique involves spraying trees with fox urine and skunk essence. Walking past the trees outside, you would barely notice the offensive smell; but if the trees are taken into a warm, closed-in living room, the smell becomes overbearing!

Another deterrent is used by Cornell University right before Christmastime: they spray their trees with a mix of red food coloring and hydrated lime, which gives the trees a decidedly non-festive fluorescent pink glow!

You Won't Believe Your Eyes

Imagine driving through a neighborhood to check out holiday lights and finding a surprising scene: what looks like a gigantic Christmas tree bursting through the roof of a house!

That's exactly the look that Aidan Walters decided to create at his family's home in Portland, Oregon. Walters, along with his father, Scott, and sister, Lauren, went to a local tree farm to choose their yearly tree, and Walters was thrilled when he found out that any tree, no matter the height, was $40. So the trio chose the tallest tree they could find, and managed to wrangle it back to the family home.

Then Walters simply cut the top of the tree off, making sure the bottom part was the same height as his living room ceiling. The top of the tree was anchored to the roof directly above the living room, and *voila!* A hilarious optical illusion was born!

A Stiff Competition

In 2014, the city of Reading, Pennsylvania put up what some people considered the world's ugliest Christmas tree. The sparsely branched, 50-foot pine drew many comparisons to the spindly tree in A Charlie Brown Christmas, although some residents felt it was even worse. "I think Charlie Brown has a better tree than we do," one citizen observed. "Everybody that took part in bringing this tree here should get fired."

In the town's defense, the "ugly" tree wasn't the original choice. A much more appealing tree had been chosen from a nearby farm, but when a crew drove out to retrieve it, the ground was too wet for a truck to drive through. So the town went to a local ballpark and chopped down the sparse, ugly tree.

After a debate between city council members, the mayor decided that the tree would stay, ugly or not. The reason? The unattractive tree garnered national attention, drawing visitors to the town of Reading— just in time for extra Christmas revenue!

A Rainbow of Trees

Are you tired of your fresh-cut Christmas tree looking so green? Sad that only artificial trees come in colors like purple and orange? Well, you're in luck—because more and more fresh-cut tree farms are offering trees in unnatural colors for the holidays!

Tree farms around the country have been embracing the trend of colorful Christmas trees, using special dyeing processes to create trees of many colors for their clients. Customers at Battaglia Christmas Tree Farm in San Martin, California, have requested blue, purple, pink, and black trees. One San Francisco 49ers fan even requested a red and gold tree!

According to Jack Keilman Trees in Johnsontown, Pennsylvania, the spray dye used on fresh trees actually helps to preserve the needles. So go ahead and enjoy a rainbow-colored tree—the dye keeps it looking fresh into the New Year and beyond!

The Grinch Had Nothing on the Adelgid

There's an ongoing war on Christmas in West Virginia. No, it has nothing to do with politicians or political correctness: this war is waged by bugs!

A tiny insect called the balsam woolly adelgid likes to chomp down on trees in the Canaan Valley National Wildlife Refuge. The refuge is home to two of the most popular Christmas tree varieties, Canaan and Fraser firs. When the bugs attack the trees, they lose the bright green color and fresh pine scent everyone longs for in a Christmas tree. If enough of the insects feed off the tree, it can become deformed and eventually die.

But don't worry if you buy your annual tree from a farm—farm-grown trees are treated with insecticide to keep the uninvited critters at bay. And even wild trees are safer in more northern climates, as the bugs can't survive in extreme cold. Santa was smart to live at the North Pole!

The Sacrifices We Make

If you love seemingly endless strings of Christmas lights but you also love really fast Wi-Fi speeds, you may have to choose between the two this holiday season. According to experts, all those twinkling decorations could slow down your connection speeds.

Daniel Carpini, who helps develop interference-resistant wireless communications for the company xG Technology, admits there's a risk. "Yeah, it's possible that your Christmas lights will have some effect on your router and broadband performance," he says.

Fortunately, the energy emitted by Christmas lights is so small that most of us are unlikely to really notice a difference—unless you literally wrap lights around your Wi-Fi router!

But Wi-Fi enabled controllers and switches for lights and decorations could also slow down speeds, so it's always a good idea to turn everything off when not in use. No reason to risk slow Wi-Fi when you're gathered around the tree watching *Elf* clips on YouTube!

Big Business

Have you ever seen a neighborhood filled with elaborately decorated houses at Christmastime and wondered how the homeowners had the time to create such intricate scenes? Well, it turns out that the war for the best light display in the neighborhood is now big business!

Companies around the country—including Mechanical Displays in Brooklyn, New York, Got Lights in Austin, Texas, and Randy's Holiday Lighting in Miami, Florida—charge big bucks for the kind of holiday displays that would make *Christmas Vacation*'s Clark Griswold proud.

Some neighborhoods, like the Dyker Heights neighborhood of Brooklyn, have gotten so wrapped up in the holiday competition that police must direct traffic and create parking areas for all the tour buses that drive to the area.

The most elaborate displays, which often feature animation and a multitude of colors, occasionally have donation boxes for viewers. The donations are then given to charity at the end of the holiday season.

Novel Christmas Ornaments

Christmas wouldn't be Christmas without the tree in Rockefeller Center. In 2016, the 94-foot-tall Norway spruce was wrapped with five miles of multicolored lights, and topped with a star made of 25,000 Swarovski crystals.

But the city of Montreal, Quebec, didn't want the New York City tree to get all the attention over the holidays. So they attempted to erect a Christmas tree that would be the tallest in North America. Unfortunately, the tree ended up standing six feet shorter than the Rockefeller Center tree. Not only that, but the tree, which was placed in the Quartier des Spectacles at Place des Arts, was spindly, sparse, and lopsided, with residents calling it "embarrassing."

But perhaps worst of all were the tree's decorations. Unlike the miles of twinkling lights and sparkling crystals adorning the New York City tree, the Montreal tree was decorated with logos for automotive parts store Canadian Tire!

When Christmas Gets "Artistic"

Claridge's, London's five-star luxury hotel, is known for its elaborate yearly Christmas tree. Past trees have been created by Dolce & Gabbana, who created a colorful tree with glass ornaments and international flags, and Christopher Bailey of Burberry, who decorated a tree with metallic umbrellas and motion-sensor lights.

But the tree in the swanky hotel's lobby in 2016 was decidedly unique—it didn't have a single light, ornament, or decoration. It was really just, well, a tree!

Instead of the usual Christmas tree, Apple designers Sir Jony Ive and Marc Newson created an "immersive festive installation." Surrounding the unadorned tree were light boxes that projected black and white images of snow-covered birch and fir trees, and the ceiling was covered in a canopy of pine branches. The design duo said that the installation aimed to "create an all-enveloping magical experience." But maybe they just ran out of ornaments and lights!

An Endless Battle

While the holidays are mostly about joy and goodwill, there is one holiday decision that remains a point of contention between tree-trimmers and home decorators: white lights, or colored lights?

It seems like a simple question, but people have very strong opinions about the issue, as Twitter makes evident. Twitter user Felicity Disco tweeted, "The only TRUE Christmas tree lights are multicolored opaque incandescent bulbs." Whereas user Lucy tweeted, "if your tree has multicolored lights I hope it burns down." Yikes.

So what does an expert say? HGTV decorator Marianne Canada says she prefers colorful lights on her own tree. "There is something about the dreariness of winter that I find the colorful lights really cheery," she says.

But really, there's no "right" answer when it comes to which palette is more aesthetically pleasing. Most people are simply drawn to the kind of lights they grew up with!

"They voted for colored lights. Now we must fight!"

Get in a Good Swim

One of the most unusual Christmas trees in the world is located in Macedonia in Eastern Europe. It's not the tallest or the biggest or even the most colorful—but it is underwater!

For more than 20 years, divers from the Amfora divers club have decorated a tree located in the Bay of Bones in Lake Ohrid. The icy lake is located within the mountainous border between Macedonia and Albania, and is one of the deepest and oldest lakes in Europe. The unique Christmas tree is located just offshore, at a depth of about 13 feet, and can be seen from the top of the clear lake.

The divers even swim down to the tree on New Year's Eve to ring in the new year, where they pass around a bottle of underwater champagne!

The decorations on the tree are dedicated to children with rare diseases; and the rarity of the underwater Christmas tree is a perfect tribute.

Santa loved the idea of an underwater tree, but it took forever for his beard to dry afterwards.

Bet You Can't Buy Just One

Even if you love decorating for the holidays, chances are you don't love it as much as Bill and Darlene Kummer, of Sheboygan, Wisconsin. After moving from a small home to a larger place with high ceilings and extra bedrooms, the couple decided their usual small tree looked out of place. So they bought a nine-foot tree to complement the soaring ceiling, and moved the smaller tree into another room of the house.

After that, the decorations started to snowball. The couple now decorates 20 Christmas trees every year, which they display in almost every room of their house. Each room is decorated with a different theme and given a unique name. There are snowflakes and polar bears in the "winter wonderland" basement, a "gingersnap" theme in the kitchen, and even a Green Bay Packers-themed tree in the study.

All the planning and decorating takes time: the Kummers begin the process in October, and don't finish until the first week of December!

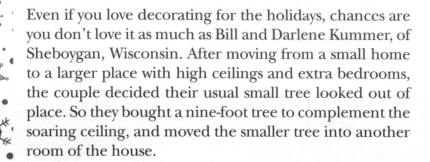

At the Store and Under the Tree

Christmas gifts: they're good, they're bad, and sometimes they're just plumb ugly. We'll explore some interesting ones that have been given and received in this chapter.

"Thank you. So very, very much."

From Putin to Popcorn

Did you receive a strange gift this Christmas that left you scratching your head over the gift-giver's intentions? Then log on to Twitter and join the club, where confused gift recipients have been posting about their unusual presents.

For instance, Paul Veal posted a picture of a Russian calendar with the comment "Straight to the top of the 'weird present' chart, yup the 2017 Putin calendar." Who wouldn't want to be regaled with a different Putin picture every month?

Eileen Shaw showed the Twitterverse a picture of a bag of popcorn. Which seems normal enough, until you read the description: "infused with 5% gin and 5% tonic." As Shaw tweeted, "This must be a contender for oddest Xmas present—'Crisp Gin & Tonic Popcorn'—what a weird concept!"

Other weird presents included a "burger pillow," a keychain featuring a cat wrapped up like sushi, and, perhaps most bizarre, a box containing the recipient's baby teeth!

Next Year, Try the Large Leather Wrapped Stone

Looking for a perfect (and extremely unusual) Christmas gift for that special someone? Then check out Nordstrom's "medium leather wrapped stone." The item is, quite literally, a stone wrapped in leather. And yes, Nordstrom really does sell them!

The stones cost $85, which seems like a steep price for something you could grab out of your backyard. Then again, according to the Nordstrom website, each stone is a "smooth Los Angeles-area stone" and they are "wrapped in rich, vegetable-tanned American leather secured by sturdy contrast backstitching." Makes the price totally worth it, right?

The best part of the stone's listing on the Nordstrom site is the hilarious comments, like the one posted by "Kenrich274": "With a lineage going back to the Stone Age, I consider myself a true rock connoisseur. And boy does this one deliver the goods. Big time. Buy now!"

You Won't See Many of These Under the Tree

Do you have tens of thousands to spend on that special someone this Christmas? How about giving a car for Christmas? And if not just any car will do, Neiman Marcus has your answer.

In its 2016 *Christmas Book* catalog, the department store featured a couple extravagant offerings for car lovers. Those looking for a perfect gift could choose a limited-edition 2017 Infinity Q60 painted in a "Solar Mica" finish, which gives the car the appearance of being gold-plated. The $63,000 car also comes with a cashmere-lined cover—so even if you're not warm in the middle of winter, your gold car will be!

Another option is the "Island Car": an open-topped electric car available in eye-popping hues of pink and green, that also come with coordinated towels, tote bags, and clothing. The $65,000 cars can only run at low speeds, and look a bit like garish golf carts. Perfect for that person who "has everything"!

I'm going to go out a limb and say
Chirpy will like this gift.

From Gift to Collection

Many people set out a snow globe or two at Christmastime for a little festive décor. But Wendy Suen, from Shanghai, China, has more than 4,000 to choose from!

Suen holds the Guinness World Record for the largest collection of snow globes. At last count, she had exactly 4,059 of the frosty-looking knickknacks throughout her home. The collector says that snow globes are symbols of "romance, dreams, and happiness," and she feels happiest when she adds a new globe to her growing collection.

Of the thousands of globes in the collection, 439 are Christmas-themed, featuring Santa Claus, Christmas trees, snowmen, and reindeer. But Suen says her favorite snow globe will always be the very first one in her collection, which was a Christmas present from her husband back in 2000.

Now, the hobbyist can walk through her very own winter wonderland any time of the year!

Just a Suggestion

Not sure what to get the man in your life? Follow humorist Dave Barry's advice: "If you want to give a man something practical, consider tires. More than once, I would have gladly traded all the gifts I got for a new set of tires."

"Wow. Socks again."

Worse Than Socks?

What's the worst gift you can give someone? According to Johnny Carson, "the worst gift is a fruitcake. There is only one fruitcake in the entire world, and people keep sending it to each other."

These Won't All Fit Under the Tree

A 36-year-old mom from the Isle of Man went viral in 2015 when she posted online a picture of her Christmas tree nearly buried under the pile of gifts she bought for her children. Emma Tapping, who writes a blog about thrifty living and saving money called *The Boss Mum*, bought her three children around 300 presents. The picture of the nearly buried Christmas tree drew lots of criticism, with many people decrying her "materialism" and accusing her of "spoiling" her kids.

But Tapping says Christmas is the only time her kids are spoiled. "They get their necessities, their school uniforms, the things that they need, but we don't go on holidays abroad, they don't go on big shopping sprees," she says. Instead, she saves and plans throughout the year to give her kids a big Christmas.

And in 2016, she defied her critics and bought even more gifts—about 350! Opening all those gifts can be a bit tricky, Tapping admits. "It's a bit like Jenga—if you pull the wrong one out you might lose a child for a few hours."

Ho Ho Ho

Darth Vader and Luke Skywalker got together for the holidays.

"I know what you're getting for Christmas," Vader said.

"How do you know?" asked Luke.

"Because," Vader replied, "I can feel your presents."

Did You Know?

An encouraging survey in Canada found that far more people prefer to give gifts—87 percent—than receive them—a mere 13 percent. It's good to know the holiday spirit is alive and well!

Ways to Spend Your Holiday Bonus

Looking for last minute gifts? Have an extra million burning a hole in your pocket? Then look no further than the annual Neiman Marcus *Christmas Book*. The catalog, which debuted in 1959, is famous for its "fantasy" gifts: extravagant items with equally extravagant price tags.

Past fantasy gifts have included a 12-day trip to India for $400,000; a motorcycle designed by Keanu Reeves for $120,000; or, for those who have even more to spend, a chance to travel to Africa and choose your own diamond. The price for that experience? A mere $1.85 million.

But don't worry—there are plenty of gifts for us mere mortals, as well, including mugs, socks, pajamas, and hot cocoa mixes. Still, Neiman Marcus president and chief merchandising officer Jim Gold says he's "often asked if we really do sell fantasy gifts. Yes, we do!"

Those Drummers Are Expensive!

Have you ever wondered how much it would cost to treat your true love to all the gifts featured in "The Twelve Days of Christmas"? Well, wonder no more: every year, PNC Bank publishes its "Christmas Price Index," which lists the cost of each of the unusual gifts in the song, along with the price difference from the previous year.

For instance, in 2016, the price for 12 drummers drumming was $2,934.10—an increase of 2.8 percent from 2015. But the cost of a partridge in a pear tree was down 2.3 percent from 2015's cost, to $209.99. Apparently, drummers are in more demand than game birds!

And remember, most of the gifts are given away multiple times, bringing the total number of gifts to 364. And the 2016 cost of all those birds, golden rings, dancers, and musicians? A whopping $156,507.88. That's a lot of true love!

"Honestly, I was hoping for ten lords a leaping?"

Layaway Angels

There's a heartwarming trend that occurs every year around holiday time, when cash-strapped parents who want to give their kids a great Christmas buy gifts on layaway. "Layaway angels" surreptitiously show up at stores and pay off layaway balances. The best part? The people they help are often total strangers!

Layaway angels have been seen at stores all around the country, sometimes paying thousands of dollars at a time to take care of strangers' bills. While most of them choose to stay anonymous, some, like Steve and Samantha Bryson of Long Beach, California, come out of the woodwork to encourage others to do the same. While the Brysons were travelling in 2016, they paid off $30,000 in layaway items at a Memphis Walmart, and also paid off $20,000 at a Kmart near Detroit.

One shopper who showed up at Pennsylvania store to pay off her merchandise was "stunned" when she found out someone had already paid. "Whoever it is is really generous. They are like the real Santa."

"I bet you can't guess what it is."

The Challenges of Technology

Some people might react with annoyance if they were inundated on Twitter with hundreds of messages meant for someone else. But John Lewis, a computer science educator from Blacksburg, Virginia, is a remarkably good sport.

Lewis shares his name with British department store John Lewis, whose Twitter handle is @johnlewisretail. The human Lewis, who uses @johnlewis, received an influx of tweets around the holidays that were meant for the store. Instead of ignoring them or closing down his Twitter account, Lewis often tweeted humorous, tongue-in-cheek responses, always adding the store's correct handle.

After realizing that one man had been getting so many tweets meant for the store, John Lewis (the department store) sent John Lewis (the man) a package full of gifts. "This is our busiest time of the year," the store said in a statement. "And we know that although he's not a retail store it can be busy for John too."

Mensch on a Bench

We've all heard of the popular "Elf on a Shelf." But what about the "Mensch on a Bench"? The Hanukkah-themed toy was created by Neal Hoffman, a Jewish father who wanted to give his kids an alternative to the Christmas toy.

And the Mensch on a Bench isn't the only unique item aimed at those who celebrate Hanukkah. How about an Emoji Menorah, which features a different expression at the base of each candle? Or you might like a "Yamaclaus," which combines Hanukkah with Christmas in a red and white Santa-hat yarmulke. These are just a couple of the items aimed at the Hanukkah market during a season that mostly focuses on Christmas.

And Hoffman isn't stopping with his Mensch on a Bench. In 2016, he created the "Ask Bubbe" doll, which is marketed as a cross between a Jewish grandmother and a Magic 8 ball.

Santa's Sleigh Isn't the Only Thing in the Air

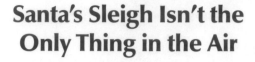

2016 brought a new, high-tech trend in Christmas gifts: drones. Around 1.2 million of the flying, remote-controlled devices were sold around the holidays, many of them bought for less than $100 at places like Walmart and Amazon.

But after opening their gifts on Christmas morning, many new drone owners faced another trend: losing or destroying their drones! The unfortunate incidents are often recorded in hilarious Twitter messages, such as the one user Greg Hillis posted on Christmas Day: "Someday I imagine my son will think about this day, the day on which I lost his brand new drone somewhere in a tree, & laugh. Someday."

Even racecar driver Dale Earnhardt Jr. got in on the Twitter drone talk, tweeting, "Shoutout to everybody who lost their Christmas drone already."

And it's no wonder—these "toys" can top speeds of 40 m.p.h. and be hard for novices to control. Maybe next year, everyone should just go back to remote control cars!

Santa's a traditionalist at heart, but he's still excited by what he's heard about this newfangled drone technology.

What Does Dad Want?

Sporting goods can be popular gift items every year. Many an active kid has loved finding a baseball glove or basketball under the tree on Christmas morning. But an unexpected item became the top sporting good sold during the 2016 holiday season: golf balls.

But not just any golf balls—the most popular golf balls sold throughout the season were Costco's store brand, Kirkland Signature. While most decent golf balls cost around $45 for a dozen, the money-saving Costco balls retail for just $29.99 for two dozen. Golfers claim that the bargain brand balls are comparable to expensive premium brands, which adds to their popularity.

And they were certainly popular for the Christmas season. After the golf balls sold out on Costco's website, the restocked balls sold out again just two hours later. This prompted some amusing online memes, such as the one Golf Unfiltered posted on Instagram: "Like Tickle Me Elmo for your dad."

Ho Ho Ho

Political satirist P.J. O'Rourke reminds us: "Christmas begins about the first of December with an office party and ends when you finally realize what you spent, around April fifteenth of the next year."

Lucking Out in the Secret Santa Swap

Most of us don't get too excited over Secret Santa gifts. They're generally modest items given by friends or co-workers, who don't always put a lot of thought into whatever they buy. But what if your Secret Santa was billionaire Bill Gates?

For several years, Gates has participated in Reddit's Secret Santa gift exchange, where one lucky Reddit user ends up with a box of Gates-approved gifts tailored to their interests. In 2016, the surprised recipient was a woman whose user name is Aerrix, who immediately took to the website to show off her impressive holiday haul.

Gates sent Aerrix about 10 gifts total, which included an XBox plus three wireless controllers and games, mittens featuring video-game character Zelda (and booties for her dog!), and DVD movies. To top it all off, Gates included a framed version of Aerrix's Reddit profile picture, in which he photoshopped himself next to her, her husband and her dog!

To Market We Go

If you like to follow the stock market, you may have noticed that it tends to do well around Christmastime. The market has an 80 percent chance of rising between the two days before Christmas and the first week of January. So does the holiday have anything to do with it?

According to experts, it's very probable. In fact, the evidence has been around for centuries. When Christmas became a public holiday in the U.K. in 1835, it began a pattern of year-end stock market strength. And the same thing happened in the U.S., when Christmas became a national holiday in 1870: a strong year-end stock market became more pronounced.

Experts have even noticed that countries which don't celebrate Christmas, but celebrate holidays at other times of the year, have stronger markets during their own holiday seasons.

So indulge in some extra celebration this year—your investments will no doubt be doing the same!

Who Needs Gold, Frankincense, or Myrrh?

A seven-year old was asked what presents the wise men brought to Jesus. He replied, "I don't know… but a Lego set would have been better." Hey, everyone loves Legos!

What Do Kids Want Anyway?

It can be difficult to find just the right gift for your child at Christmas. The average parent spends about 16 days searching for presents during the holiday season. And according to experts, 13-year-olds cause their parents the most anxiety—they're the toughest to shop for!

According to research done by British retail store Tesco, younger children are easier to shop for and more readily share their wishes for presents. Seven-year-olds write longer wish lists than kids of any other age, with an average of 11 items. The more items on the list, the easier it is for parents to shop!

Thirteen-year-olds not only provide shorter wish lists, but parents say that teens of that age constantly change their minds about what they like. And 30 percent of parents worry that their young teens will grow bored with their gifts quickly.

Perhaps a gift card or good old fashioned cash is the best decision!

Pint-Sized Fashion

The 2016 Christmas season featured a surprising fashion icon: three-year-old Prince George of Cambridge. The pint-sized royal wore a gray wool coat from Spanish clothing retailer Pepa & Co. to a holiday church service with his famous parents, Prince William and Princess Kate, and fashion-conscious parents everywhere took notice.

After being spotted in the coat at the church in Princess Kate's hometown of Bucklebury, orders for the outerwear began pouring in to the online retailer. The coat, which cost approximately $147, sold out within hours!

This wasn't the first time that the adorable prince caused online shoppers to grab their credit cards. Many of the prince's outfits have been popular with parents around the world, from the blankets he was wrapped in as a baby, to the pajamas he wore when meeting President Obama. No doubt there will be many fashionable toddlers sporting their "royal" garments this holiday season!

In the Mail

Every year, Americans sent Christmas cards and gifts through the mail. Let's look at some of those cards and stories.

The wrong picture went out with the Christmas cards that year...

Christmas Card Controversy!

Have you ever wondered what the very first Christmas card was like? The idea for a holiday card was developed by Sir Henry Cole, who was a post office worker in the U.K. in 1843. He asked his artist friend, John Horsley, to design a card, which was then printed and sold for one shilling each.

The card was printed with the words "A Merry Christmas and a Happy New Year to you," and had three panels. The outer panels featured images of people caring for the poor, and the middle panel showed a family enjoying a holiday dinner.

But some people complained about the festive card: because in the middle of that family dinner, there is a small child, and an adult is holding a glass of wine to the young person's lips. Yes, the very first Christmas card featured a child drinking alcohol!

A MERRY CHRISTMAS
AND
A HAPPY NEW YEAR
TO YOU

Published at Summerly's Home Treasury Office
12 Old Bond Street, London.

From

THE FIRST CHRISTMAS CARD (1846), DESIGNED BY J. C. HORSLEY, R.A., FOR SIR HENRY COLE

Can you spot the tipsy child in the very first Christmas card?

Naughty or Nice?

Many of us send Christmas cards to friends and family every holiday season. But the police chief of the Abbotsford Police Department near Vancouver, Canada, takes a different approach: every year, the department sends out Christmas cards to criminals!

The cards, which have been sent out every year since 2012, are mailed to known drug dealers, gang members, and vandals, in the hopes that their message will cause the criminals to reflect on their behavior. The 2012 card featured Police Chief Bob Rich dressed as Santa, wearing a bulletproof vest and helmet, with the message, "Which list will you be on next year?" Subsequent cards have included messages like, "Where will you be spending the holidays this season? We hope it is with your family, not us."

The cards even include a number to call for those who wish to confess crimes or turn their lives around, and many recipients have made use of it, hopefully resulting in a future of much happier holidays!

"I'm so cute that my parents can't choose just one picture for the Christmas card cover!"

Lost in the Mail

We all feel a little harried around the holidays, but one postal worker in Queens, New York, went too far when he tried to lighten his workload.

Daniel Darby, who worked in the Ozone Park neighborhood of Queens, felt "overwhelmed" by the holiday-season mail and packages he was forced to deliver. So he stopped by a store one December evening and bought three garbage bags. He then stuffed all the extra mail into the bags and left them in a residential garbage can, where they were discovered a few days later.

And Darby wasn't the only crooked courier during the holiday season. James Hayden, who delivered mail in Brooklyn, admitted to opening Christmas mail and stealing gift cards. He was even caught on surveillance camera using one of the cards, while still wearing his mailman uniform!

Both postal workers are now facing up to five years in prison for their Christmas crimes.

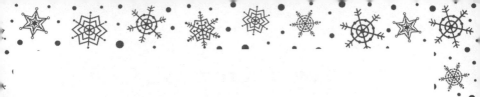

Ho Ho Ho

Be sure to heed Johnny Carson's advice when sending out Christmas gifts: "Mail your packages early so the post office can lose them in time for Christmas."

A Unique Christmas Card

Sometimes it seems like the holidays are only about couples, families, and kids. For single people, Christmas can be a bit alienating. Take holiday cards, for instance. Every year, our mailboxes are filled with cards from family and friends, who include plenty of pictures of weddings, vacations, and their kids' milestones. But what sort of card can a single person send to set herself apart?

Sarah Collins, a 28-year-old single woman, answered that question with her 2016 Christmas card. In it, she poses with her true love: pizza. She even added a "sonogram" picture of a slice of *in utero* pizza!

"I chose pizza because it always answers my calls, comforts me when I need it, and gives my stomach a warm hug," Collins said about her Christmas card partner.

And lest anyone wonder where the singleton's stereotypical cats are, Collins promises "that's next year's card."

"I'm not sure if this is my best angle."

Smells Good!

In 2004, the German post office gave away 20 million scratch-n-sniff stickers so people could make their Christmas cards smell like pine, cinnamon, gingerbread, or honey!

"Just take the picture already. I've got a busy schedule of pooping and rolling over to get back to."

Did You Know?

Fun fact: The U.S. Postal Service delivers 20 billion cards and packages between Thanksgiving and Christmas Eve. They certainly give Santa a run for his money!

Peace on Earth, Good Will Towards...Most?

Christmas brings about tales of heartwarming generosity—but also strife. It's a time for families, who can be a blessing—or a stressor. If you're down this Christmas, you can at least console yourself with the idea that someone, somewhere, is having a worse time.

A Bit of Neighborhood Conflict

The lights, decorations, and songs of the holiday season add to the cheer and magic of Christmas. But even the biggest holiday lover can turn into a Grinch after hearing the same rendition of "Jingle Bells" over and over. Case in point: New York lawyer Nick Wilder sued his neighbor, Lisa Maria Falcone, in 2016 in an effort to end the non-stop music blaring from her imposing Christmas display.

Falcone owns three townhouses across the street from Wilder's apartment, which were decked out in lights and decorations for the holiday season. The display also included nonstop music, which, according to Wilder, played from 7 a.m. until midnight every day of the festive season. "I like a Christmas song on Christmas Day," Wilder said. "But I'm tired of hearing 'Jingle Bells' like 700 or 800 times a day."

All Wilder wanted for Christmas was for his neighbor to "show some Christmas spirit by being considerate and stop annoying the entire neighborhood."

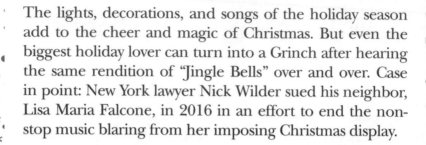

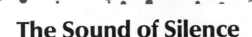

The Sound of Silence

Talk about a Christmas Scrooge: A shop owner in Portsmouth, New Hampshire, called police to complain about the noise made by a Salvation Army bell ringer. The charity's annual donation kettles have been around since 1891, and it's common to see the familiar red kettles and bell ringers outside of shops and businesses throughout the holiday season.

But Sarah Hamilton-Parker is tired of the ringing bells. "I listen to this for 200 hours a year," she said. "I don't get a break. It makes my blood pressure go sky high."

Hamilton-Parker tried to convince police that the bell-ringers were violating the city's noise ordinance, but local police say the fund raisers are given special permission to make extra noise on a seasonal basis.

So for now, all the grumpy shop owner can do is wear a pair of earplugs and wait for the new year, when the pesky charity will go quiet—until next season!

Just When You Thought You Were Safe

A New Jersey man sued the owners of an apartment building after tripping over a hazard: a discarded Christmas tree.

Kyu Taik Chung was walking along a sidewalk outside the building when he encountered the tree, which he claims was "recklessly, carelessly and/or negligently" left in a location which made the walkway hazardous. According to his attorney, Albert H. Wunsch III, Chung was so badly injured that he hasn't been able to work or live a normal life. And medical bills resulting from what Wunsch calls "severe and permanent injuries" have been stacking up.

In Chung's defense, the date of his alleged injury—March 12—does raise some questions. Why did someone wait until March to throw away their Christmas tree? And should pedestrians anticipate a discarded tree on the sidewalk when spring flowers have already started to bloom?

Hopefully both parties in this Christmas case have learned a lesson!

Did You Know?

According to an analysis of Facebook posts, one of the most popular times for couples to break up is two weeks before Christmas. Fortunately, Christmas Day is the least popular day to break up!

Better or Worse Than Regular Jet Lag?

Many of us gather together with extended family at the holidays, and spend days with relatives we rarely see. Huge meals are cooked, gifts are exchanged, small talk is made. But afterwards, when we finally return to the peace and quiet of our own lives, we often feel completely exhausted. Turns out, psychologists have a term for this: family jet lag!

Just like regular jet lag, family jet lag occurs because of a disruption in a usual routine. But you don't even have to travel to experience it: if you were the one hosting all those out-of-town visitors, the stress and pressure of accommodating guests is enough to make you feel as if you took a red-eye flight across the country.

To counter the effects, psychologists suggest getting more sleep, learning to say no when necessary, and staying in a hotel if it's more comfortable than being around family 24/7.

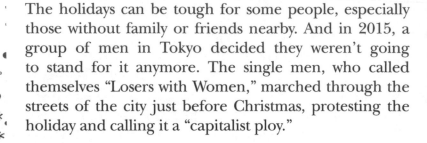

Losing the Christmas Spirit

The holidays can be tough for some people, especially those without family or friends nearby. And in 2015, a group of men in Tokyo decided they weren't going to stand for it anymore. The single men, who called themselves "Losers with Women," marched through the streets of the city just before Christmas, protesting the holiday and calling it a "capitalist ploy."

According to the "Losers," Christmas is nothing but a consumerist holiday that preys on "people in love," because "happy people support capitalism." They also used their Christmastime rally to denounce the "discrimination" that single men face.

In their defense, Christmas is not an official holiday in Japan, so it is celebrated more as a romantic holiday for couples. The "Losers" have also protested Valentine's Day and other Western holidays in past marches. Sounds like someone needs a girlfriend!

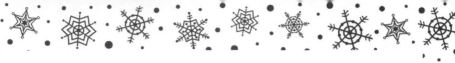

Maybe Just Go to a Restaurant

A woman in the U.K. took to the internet to ask for some holiday advice. Her question? She wanted to know if it was unreasonable to charge her own family for a Christmas dinner she offered to host!

In her defense, the woman said she and her husband had fallen on some hard financial times, and although she was more than willing to do "the bulk of everything" she requested £5 from each family member.

Users of the parenting website Mumsnet, where the woman posted her question, weren't too sympathetic to her financial woes. "Don't offer to host if you can't afford it," one user chided. Another said, "You are being unreasonable, you are not a restaurant." But some users offered helpful suggestions, such as hosting a potluck instead of providing all of the food.

No word on how the woman's Christmas dinner turned out, but family tension is nothing new during the holidays!

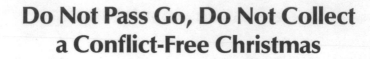

Do Not Pass Go, Do Not Collect a Conflict-Free Christmas

The holidays can be full of stressful situations. From overdone turkeys, to houses full of loud relatives, to frantically wrapping last-minute gifts. But there's another, seemingly innocuous, situation that causes strife to families everywhere: playing Monopoly.

Yes, the beloved board game, which has been in homes since the 1930s, is known to cause so many arguments and disagreements between players that the U.K. division of Hasbro offered a special Christmas hotline in 2016.

A survey found that more than half of Monopoly games end in arguments, with the most common complaint being that players make up the rules as they go along. So the game experts answering phones for the hotline, which ran from December 24 to December 26, had official rulebooks on hand to settle disagreements.

But perhaps, for the sake of family harmony, it would be better to forgo the game and simply watch *It's a Wonderful Life*.

You'd Think It Would Be Too Cold to Fight

The combination of holiday stress, boisterous celebration, and alcohol can lead to some unusual Christmastime confrontations. Take, for instance, a fight that broke out between two men on Christmas Day in 2007. Although the fight itself was not so unusual, the two brawlers had to be airlifted from an unusual location: the Amundsen-Scott South Pole station in Antarctica!

News of the fight reached McMurdo station, the headquarters for the U.S. Antarctic Program, which is about 850 miles away. Workers at McMurdo had been looking forward to a day off for the Christmas holiday, but had to dispatch a plane to the South Pole to pick up the fighters. One of the men was then flown to New Zealand, with what was suspected to be a broken jaw. The other man was flown back to the U.S.

No doubt both men were placed on Santa's naughty list!

One Way to Channel Conflict

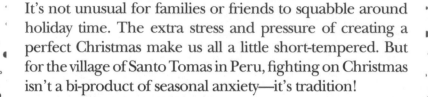

It's not unusual for families or friends to squabble around holiday time. The extra stress and pressure of creating a perfect Christmas make us all a little short-tempered. But for the village of Santo Tomas in Peru, fighting on Christmas isn't a bi-product of seasonal anxiety—it's tradition!

On Christmas morning, the entire village heads to a local bullfighting ring and participates in a festival known as *Takanakuy*. Villagers—whether men or women, young or old—pair off and start fighting. The tradition isn't entirely without reason, however: Santo Tomas is so remote that it is mostly cut off from the main resources and government services in Peru. This means a paltry police force and no easily accessible lawyers, judges, or courthouses.

So once a year, differences are settled with the *Takanakuy* festival. Surprisingly, those who lose their fights usually willingly acquiesce to the victor, and all is well for another year in Santo Tomas.

Through a Child's Eyes

Kids have a special viewpoint when it comes to the holidays. In this chapter we'll look at some stories of their unique takes on Santa, presents, and more.

Ho Ho Ho

A little girl thanked her grandfather for the violin he gave her for Christmas. "It's the best gift I've ever gotten!" she exclaimed.

"Really?" her surprised grandfather asked.

"Oh yes," said the girl. "Because every time I start playing, mom gives me two dollars to stop!"

Just Say Please

There's good news and bad news when it comes to kids writing to Santa. The good news? Many kids aren't as materialistic as we assumed they were. The bad news? They also aren't as polite!

Carole Slotterback, a psychology professor at the University of Scranton in Pennsylvania, sifted through 1,200 of the letters between 1998 and 2003 to analyze them for her book *The Psychology of Santa*. She discovered that children who wrote letters, instead of lists of requests, were more conversational and chatty.

Slotterback discovered that not all kids are as toy-crazy as we would think they'd be. Instead, many children ask for things like good health for sick relatives.

But Slotterback did note that many children failed to use the word "please" when making requests, with the exception of kids who asked for pets. In fact, one boy who asked Santa for a dog used the word 16 times in his letter!

"I couldn't find this online,
so it's up to you."

A Rhyming Problem

A boy asked his mom to make him a leopard costume for his school's nativity play. Thinking it must be a *Lion King* or *Jungle Book* theme, she asked his teacher to clarify. The amused teacher said it was a traditional nativity play, and the boy was playing a shepherd—not a leopard!

Who wouldn't want to be a Christmas leopard?

A Generous Tradition

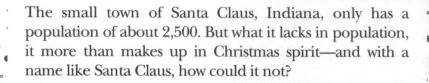

The small town of Santa Claus, Indiana, only has a population of about 2,500. But what it lacks in population, it more than makes up in Christmas spirit—and with a name like Santa Claus, how could it not?

Every year, the town is inundated with letters to Santa Claus, which the U.S. Postal Service delivers to the tiny Santa Claus Post Office. And volunteers from the small town—known as elves, naturally—take the time to handwrite responses to each one.

The tradition of writing responses to the letters began back in 1914, when the postmaster of Santa Claus, James Martin, felt bad that children were sending letters to Santa without getting a response. So he started writing back to them.

Over the years, the numbers of letters that end up in Santa Claus have grown to the tens of thousands, and dozens of "elves" in the community work to write back to each one, ensuring that children around the world believe in Christmas magic!

Ho Ho Ho

A little boy was asked to say a prayer before Christmas dinner. He bowed his head and gave thanks for each item of food on the table, from the turkey to the cranberry sauce, but then paused. He finally nudged his mom and asked, "If I thank God for the Brussels sprouts, won't he know I'm lying?"

A Fortuitous Mistake

You've probably seen NORAD's Santa Tracking System on Christmas Eve. Every year, NORAD—the North American Aerospace Defense Command—issues reports on where Santa's sleigh is located, to the delight of boys and girls everywhere. But the tradition may have never started had it not been for one misdialed phone number.

According to legend, Sears department store printed an ad in 1955, telling kids they could call Santa on his private phone line. But the number was either misprinted, or a child misdialed; somehow, a six-year-old trying to reach Santa ended up calling U.S. Air Force Colonel Harry Shoup, the director of operations at NORAD's predecessor, the Continental Air Defense Command.

But instead of hanging up on the child, Shoup decided to play Santa. And when more kids began reaching the number, Shoup, with the help of his staff, started giving them information on the whereabouts of Santa's sleigh. And the rest, as they say, is history!

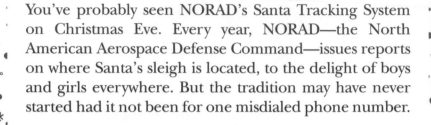

"No, you can't sue Santa
for bringing you too few gifts."

Someone Needs to Hold the Camera

Two little girls were looking at a picture of Mary holding baby Jesus. "That's Mary," said one girl, "and that's the baby Jesus in her arms."

The other girl asked, "Where's Jesus's dad then?"

The first girl replied, "Oh, he's the one taking the picture."

Christmas in Jeopardy!

If you have kids in your life, you've probably heard of the holiday story *The Elf on the Shelf,* and seen its accompanying red-bedecked stuffed figure. As the story goes, the elf watches over boys and girls and reports back to Santa about who's been naughty and who's been nice. But the elf has one rule: it must not be touched, otherwise the Christmas magic could disappear.

So when seven-year-old Isabelle LaPeruta, of Old Bridge, New Jersey, accidentally hit her Elf on the Shelf with a bouncing ball, she panicked. The little girl dialed 911, and tearfully told the operator that she was afraid she'd ruined Christmas. When her mother, Lynanne, awoke from a nap, she found her crying daughter with a police officer, and had a talk about what constitutes an emergency.

But kudos to the Old Bridge Police Department, who understood Isabelle's panic: "To her, it was an emergency," said Lt. Joseph Mandola. "In her mind, she did right, and it was fine with us."

"Someday I'm going to grow up to be Santa!"

Ho Ho Ho

A little boy was in his yard one holiday season, yelling, "I wish I had a new bike for Christmas!"

A neighbor walking by heard him and said, "What's all the noise? Santa Claus isn't deaf, you know."

The little boy said, "No, but my Aunt Jane is!"

"We have a strategy for getting the presents we want and it involves maximum cuteness. "

Adorable Animals

Our furry family members play an integral part in our Christmas celebrations.

"I think it's a good look for me!"

"Remember, we don't beg.
We make a list."

All I Want for Christmas

A Florida man and his cat, Misty, were surprised by a pet-friendly Christmas miracle in 2016. Cat-owner Jonathan was devastated when Misty disappeared in October, but after weeks of searching for her with no luck, he decided to head to the Jacksonville Humane Society and adopt a new feline friend.

The humane society thought they had the perfect cat for the distraught cat lover. "Bon Bon"—a pretty tortoiseshell-colored cat—had been at the shelter for months. Although she was very sweet, no one seemed to want to adopt her.

The staff couldn't understand why until Jonathan saw her: Bon Bon was his own tortoiseshell cat, Misty! As far as everyone at the humane society was concerned, it was simply holiday magic that brought the two back together. And human and cat were able to enjoy Christmas together again!

"An intruder came down the chimney, but I fought him off and won this trophy! Aren't you proud?"

Let Them Eat Cake

If you're one of those people who treats their dog like family, then head to Japan for Christmas. Lucky dogs get to share in their owner's holiday festivities and enjoy their very own dog-friendly Christmas cake.

Pastry chef Naohiko Nagatani created a new version of Japan's holiday confection, which is made with sponge cake and covered with whipped cream, to make it safe for man's best friend. He made sure there was no chocolate or alcohol in the recipe, and uses spelt flour instead of regular flour because it is less likely to cause allergies.

Maybe it seems strange to share your Christmas sweets with your dog, but Nagatani says it's just the way things are in his country. "The birth rate's declining here in Japan, so dogs have pretty much become like children and people want to share Christmas with them," he explains.

And who can say no to a furry friend begging for cake?

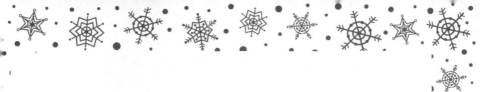

"I don't know why the adults keep putting
things on our heads, do you?"

"We've got our Christmas finery on
and we're ready to go!"

"I. Want. That. Hat."

"All this shopping and wrapping and
decorating gets exhausting!"

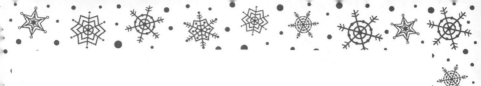

"Dear Santa, we'd like to audition to pull the sleigh. We promise we're good dogs!"

"Our selfie is cuter than yours!"

Music

From ancient carols to rock 'n' roll, traditional to cutting edge, Christmas music shapes our holidays and our memories.

A Modern Christmas Miracle

When we think of nonagenarians, we don't usually associate them with pop singer Taylor Swift. But 96-year-old Cyrus Porter is one of the singer's biggest fans. And the day after Christmas in 2016, Swift surprised the World War II veteran by showing up at his home in New Madrid, Missouri, and giving him and 60 of his family members a private concert!

Porter, who says listening to the singer helps him connect with his two dozen grandchildren, talked about his Swift fandom on a local news station just a few days earlier. Swift saw the interview, and in the true spirit of the season, she decided to give Porter and his family a Christmas surprise by singing for them in person.

Porter's grandson, Robert Frye, posted pictures and video of the surprise private concert on Twitter. "It's a Christmas miracle!!!" he tweeted. "Thank you @taylorswift13. My grandpa was so excited!!"

A Racing Song

If there's one song that you can guarantee you'll hear every holiday season, it's "Jingle Bells." The song has become synonymous with the Christmas season, and it just wouldn't feel right without it. But did you know that the song wasn't originally written for Christmas?

"Jingle Bells" was composed by James Lord Pierpont in 1850, while he was relaxing at the Simpson Tavern in Medford, Massachusetts. Nearby, residents liked to race sleighs down Salem Street to Malden Square, and this inspired Pierpont to start writing his famous tune. The song was finally published in 1857 under the title "One Horse Open Sleigh."

Although Pierpont's song was simply a fun tune about winter hijinks, it almost immediately became associated with Christmas. It also has the distinction of being the first song broadcast from space, where Gemini 6 astronauts performed for Mission Control on December 16, 1965!

From Frustration to Fame

Most of us would be rather frustrated if we missed our train to head home for the holidays. But 21-year-old Emanuele Fasano, who was traveling from Milan to Rome to spend Christmas with his family, made the most of his unfortunate situation—and it turned out to be an unexpectedly good decision!

Fasano missed his train at Milan's Centrale station, so he needed to kill some time before the next train arrived. The station features a piano that anyone may use, so the young man sat down and began to play. To the amazement of his fellow travelers, Fasano skillfully played a piece of his own composition, titled *Non so come mai*.

One of the passers-by on the platform happened to be television producer Alberto Simone, who recorded Fasano's impromptu concert and posted it on YouTube, where it's had more than three million views.

And Fasano has already had two job offers thanks to the video. He says his dream is to make a living from music. "But for now," he says, "I'm enjoying this great Christmas gift."

Ho Ho Ho

Good King Wenceslas called up his favorite pizza joint to place an order.

"Do you want your usual?" the store employee asked. "Deep pan, crisp and even?"

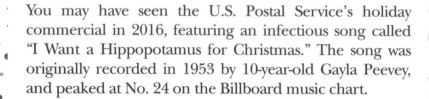

You Say Christmas, I Think Hippos

You may have seen the U.S. Postal Service's holiday commercial in 2016, featuring an infectious song called "I Want a Hippopotamus for Christmas." The song was originally recorded in 1953 by 10-year-old Gayla Peevey, and peaked at No. 24 on the Billboard music chart.

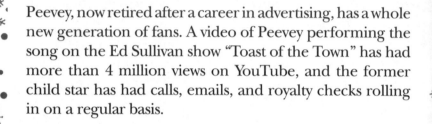

Peevey, now retired after a career in advertising, has a whole new generation of fans. A video of Peevey performing the song on the Ed Sullivan show "Toast of the Town" has had more than 4 million views on YouTube, and the former child star has had calls, emails, and royalty checks rolling in on a regular basis.

But even if you know every word of the catchy song, you may not know that Peevey's unusual Christmas wish actually came true! At Christmastime in 1953, the Central Park Zoo shipped a real, live hippo to Peevey's hometown of Oklahoma City, which she donated to her local zoo.

The next question is, what does the
hippo want for Christmas?

A Reason for Singing

We hear the Christmas standard "Rockin' Around the Christmas Tree" every year without fail. The energetic holiday tune was recorded by "I'm Sorry" singer Brenda Lee in 1958. It may not be surprising that the song is still a hit; but what is surprising is the fact that Lee was only 13 years old when she recorded it!

The diminutive singer, who was nicknamed "Little Miss Dynamite," started singing when she was only two years old. Her father died when she was eight, and by the time she was ten years old, she was the main breadwinner of her family, appearing on shows like *TV Ranch*, *The Peach Blossom Special*, and *Ozark Jubilee*. The latter would turn out to be her big break into show business, and three years later she recorded the song she's best known for—"Rockin' Around the Christmas Tree."

Although it took several years for the song to become a certifiable hit, the tune—amazingly sung by a 13-year-old!—has now sold more than 25 million copies.

Making the Work Go Easy

Getting work done on your house is seldom a pleasant experience. Especially if you happen to be remodeling your kitchen or bathroom around the stressful holiday season. But two contractors in Indiana have found a way to bring extra joy to their clients: they sing Christmas carols while hanging drywall or installing lights.

Josh Arnett and Aaron Gray have been friends since they were 13, when they began singing at their church. When they started working as contractors several years ago, the talented duo would occasionally sing songs to pass the time, to the delight of their impressed customers.

Now, Arnett and Gray are an internet sensation known as The Singing Contractors, a name given to them by their loyal clients. Singing acapella carols and hymns during the holiday season, the contractors consider their work "a ministry of sorts."

"Sometimes," Arnett says, "you need to hear a message of love and peace."

Whoops!

A church in Sri Lanka made an embarrassing mistake in the booklet for their Christmas Carol service in 2016. Instead of printing the words to the Hail Mary prayer, they ended up printing the words to late rapper Tupac's song "Hail Mary."

The profanity-laced lyrics were distributed to churchgoers who came to the "festival of music for peace and harmony." Instead of seeing the traditional prayer which begins, "Hail Mary, full of grace," parishioners were shocked to see lyrics depicting violence and using inappropriate language.

Fortunately, a few people recognized the mistake before the service began, and organizers were able to ask attendees to return the booklets, hopefully before too many people read through the words!

Father Da Silva, from the Archdiocese of Columbo, explained that a young boy had been in charge of printing the booklets, and had simply accidentally printed the incorrect lyrics. "We are very sorry to say that this happened," he apologized.

Go, NHS!

A choir made up of doctors and nurses from Great Britain's National Health Service pulled off a Christmas miracle in 2015, beating out Justin Bieber for the No. 1 song in the nation. The choir's song, called "A Bridge Over You," sold 31,000 more copies than Bieber's single "Love Yourself." Even better, all proceeds from the sale of the song went to health-related charities.

Bieber himself may have had something to do with the upset, as he urged his Twitter followers to "do the right thing" and buy the NHS Choir's song. An admirable thing to say, considering this is the same man who once made his bodyguards carry him up the Great Wall of China because he was "tired"!

But to his credit, Bieber also congratulated the NHS Choir when they were awarded the No. 1 spot, tweeting, "Amazing. This is what Christmas is all about. @Choir_NHS congrats! Very cool."

Did You Know?

Former Beatles singer Paul McCartney earns around $400,000 every year from his holiday song "Wonderful Christmastime," even though some critics consider it "the worst Christmas song ever"!

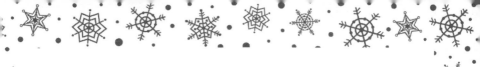

On the Screen

Let's take a fresh look at our favorite Christmas TV specials and movies, which make us laugh…and sometimes sniffle.

When in Sweden

You probably have a favorite film or Christmas special you like to watch every year: *It's a Wonderful Life*, *A Charlie Brown Christmas*, or *Home Alone*, perhaps. But residents of Sweden have a very unusual Christmas Eve television viewing tradition.

Every year since 1959, families across Sweden have stopped whatever they're doing at 3 p.m. on Christmas Eve to enjoy a viewing of the 1958 *Walt Disney Presents* Christmas special, *From All of Us to All of You*. The special features Disney cartoons from the '30s, '40s, and '50s, most of which have absolutely nothing to do with Christmas.

The special is immensely popular in the Scandinavian country, where people plan their schedule around the airtime and often half the population tunes in to watch.

And if you don't want to watch, good luck finding anything else to do. As one Swede says, on Christmas Eve "At 3 o'clock in the afternoon, you can't to do anything else, because Sweden is closed."

Did You Know?

If the costumes worn by Will Ferrell and the actors playing Santa's elves in *Elf* look familiar, it may be because they are exactly the same as the outfits worn by the stop-motion animated elves in the classic *Rudolph the Red-Nosed Reindeer*!

If You've Wondered

When watching the holiday classic *Home Alone*, viewers inevitably have some questions: How could parents not know that they'd left a child behind? How could an eight-year-old set up all those booby traps? Would the burglars actually be able to survive Kevin's house of horrors? And exactly how much did a Paris vacation for all those people cost?

Well, the last question can be answered with a bit of research. According to Kevin's mom, Kate (played by Catherine O'Hara), the trip was funded by Kevin's uncle Rob. Rob paid for 15 people to fly to France—four of them in first class. How much do four first class tickets to Paris at the holidays cost? About $43,000. And 11 coach tickets would be around $14,000.

Add to that the cost of tourist attractions and food for 15 (or, since Kevin was left behind, 14) people, and the grand total comes in at more than $58,000!

Did You Know?

The gangster movie that Kevin McCallister watches in *Home Alone* was a parody made just for the film, based on a 1938 movie called *Angels with Dirty Faces* starring James Cagney and Humphrey Bogart. The movie Kevin watches is titled *Angels with Filthy Souls*.

A "Red" Christmas?

Did you know that in 1947 some FBI analysts were concerned by the film *It's a Wonderful Life*? They said the story attempted to discredit bankers, which was a "common trick used by Communists"!

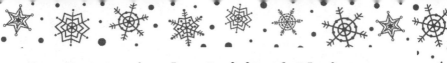

That Is Not in the Spirit of Christmas

In recent years, viewers of the holiday classic *A Charlie Brown Christmas* have been annoyed to discover that networks have trimmed scenes out of the cartoon special in order to make room for more commercials. The Emmy-winning special has always tugged at the heartstrings with its messages of simplicity and hope, and its denouncement of the over-commercialization of Christmas. So viewers were especially struck by the irony of cutting scenes about Christmas commercialization in order to air commercials!

The run time of the special is 25.5 minutes in its entirely, but networks prefer shows to have a 22-minute airtime to accommodate commercials.

But fans say cutting any of the classic scenes is going too far. Especially for a special that aims to show the true meaning of Christmas—and it isn't commercials!

Not Just a Myth

Remember the "tongue stuck to the flagpole" scene in *A Christmas Story*? The show *Mythbusters* ran tests to see if a person's tongue could actually get stuck to cold metal, and discovered that it is possible. It should go without saying, but don't lick cold flagpoles!

Learning the Hard Way

A girl in New Hampshire, who had never seen the classic *A Christmas Story*, nor presumably the *Mythbusters* episode, found out the hard way that you should never stick your tongue on an ice-cold flagpole!

Maddie Gilmartin was outside with her father, Shawn, while he was snow plowing the driveway. On impulse, she decided to see what would happen if she touched her tongue to the flag pole in the yard. Maddie said she was thinking, "it will come right off," but just like in the famous scene in the movie, her tongue stuck stubbornly to the metal.

It took her father 15 minutes to warm up the pole enough to free Maddie from the metal. Afterwards, the risk-taker said it felt "like a gang of bees" had attacked her poor mouth.

A good reminder to heed the lessons learned from *A Christmas Story*!

Behind the Scenes

If you have seen the cartoon version of Dr. Seuss's Christmas classic *How the Grinch Stole Christmas,* you've heard the distinctive voice of Boris Karloff narrating the story. The horror-film veteran's deep baritone lends a certain air of authority to the voice that admonishes the joy-stealing Grinch, especially during the famous musical number, "You're a Mean One, Mr. Grinch."

There's one problem though: Karloff didn't sing the song! The actor wasn't known for his singing prowess, so the "Grinch" production team turned to voice actor Thurl Ravenscroft to handle the musical numbers. But Ravenscroft wasn't credited for his work, leading many to believe that Karloff sang the song.

Even if the name Thurl Ravenscroft isn't familiar, you've definitely heard his voice work before: he was the famous voice of Tony the Tiger in Kellogg's Frosted Flakes television commercials. You'll probably never hear "theeey're greeeeat!" again without thinking about the Grinch!

A Burp of Art (and Other *Elf* Trivia)

The department store in the movie *Elf*, Gimbels, was a real store that existed until 1987. The exterior used for the movie was the Macy's department store on 34th Street, digitally altered to appear as Gimbels. Macy's, incidentally, was a Gimbels competitor!

Peter Billingsley, who as a child played Ralphie in *A Christmas Story*, had an uncredited cameo 20 years later in *Elf*. He played (of course) an elf in Santa's workshop.

Remember Buddy the Elf's impressive 12-second burp in *Elf*? The sound was provided by famous voice actor Maurice LaMarche, who is perhaps best known for being the voice of "The Brain" in the animated series *Animaniacs*.

Christmas Sweaters

Compared to Christmas trees or old-time carols, the Christmas sweater is a relatively new tradition, but it's brought joy to many in that time. Love may it live, in all its horrible, wonderful glory!

You know you want to host an ugly sweater party. You know you do.

Honor the Sweater

We've all seen gaudy, garish Christmas sweaters—some so outlandish we can't believe anyone would wear them. But those tacky-looking garments—which actually have their very own "holiday," National Ugly Christmas Sweater Day—can bring in big bucks! Because of the popularity of ugly Christmas sweater contests at parties and in offices around the country, people search high and low for the most unappealing attire they can find. Recognizing this unusual market, some people have taken advantage of ugly sweater popularity and started selling the garments online.

Take Florida stay-at-home mom Anne Marie Blackman, for instance. She buys ugly Christmas sweaters at thrift stores, then adds even more decoration with sequins or macramé. She sells her creations on eBay, and has made enough money to send her son to college!

So next time your great-aunt sends you a colorful sweater for Christmas, don't rush to the store to exchange it. It could be worth more than you think!

The Logical Conclusion of Ugly Sweaterhood

How much would you spend for an ugly Christmas sweater? How about $30,000? Well, if you have that kind of money to throw away, check out the "World's Most Expensive Ugly Christmas Sweater" from the Tipsy Elves website.

The sweater—which features Santa riding a unicorn past, for some reason, the planet Saturn—is covered with more than 24,000 individually placed Swarovski crystals, which took 52 hours of work to create. The gaudy sweater is shipped inside a "luxury frame," so at least no one is actually expecting the buyer to wear it.

The best part of this holiday monstrosity might be the snarky reviews it has generated on the Tipsy Elves website. User Jessica says, "I was going to fund my daughter's wedding in Cabo, but I figured this sweater would last much longer. Great value!" And James wonders, "Can someone from Tipsy Elves confirm the size of the shipping box this sweater comes in? I will need to live inside the box if I buy this sweater."

Create Your Own!

Ugly Christmas sweaters have become so mainstream that it's not difficult to find something hideous to wear to an ugly sweater party. But what if you have a more specific design in mind? Enter UglyChristmasSweater.com, where you can create your own ugly sweater!

The website sold five million dollars' worth of holiday hideousness in 2015. Their merchandise includes Star Wars-themed sweaters, pullovers with flashing LED lights, and even 3-D sweaters. But in case none of those are ugly enough, the website now has a "customize sweater" tool, which it launched in 2016.

Customers can choose a sweater color, and then add patterns like reindeer and snowflakes. They then upload their own artwork or photos to complete the look. The service is so popular that it takes three weeks for a design to be completed and shipped from China. Although one sweater costs almost $100, buying in bulk reduces the cost to $50 per sweater. You'll just need to find 100 friends who share your love of ugly Christmas sweaters!

How Did It Start?

Think back to the first time you started seeing "ugly Christmas sweaters" everywhere. Chances are, it coincides with the year the film *Bridget Jones' Diary* was released.

In the film, hapless Bridget, wearing her own "ugly" Christmas outfit, meets old friend Mark Darcy at her family's Christmas party. Mark is wearing a comically horrible outfit—a green sweater with the face of a red-nosed reindeer knitted on the front.

According to director Sharon Maguire, a lot of thought went into the choice of Mark Darcy's ugly Christmas sweater. "It had to be just right," she explained. "The character of Mr. Darcy is a constipated English prig when we first meet him so we needed something totally ridiculous to pierce that pomposity."

Since that hilarious scene, ugly holiday sweaters have become more and more popular, and continue to show up in films like 2016's *Almost Christmas* and *Office Christmas Party*.

**Runners in Vancouver embrace their
ugly sweaters in a themed 5K run.**

Sharing the Joy

The ugly sweater craze has definitely found its way into our holiday festivities in recent years. But for some people, it's not enough to see humans walking around in the horrendous garments; now pets are wearing ugly sweaters, too!

But don't worry: the festively festooned pets are wearing their holiday best (or worst!) for good causes. In Washington, D.C., the Humane Rescue Alliance holds holiday fundraisers where pet owners, like Cassidy Hart, dress up in ugly sweaters with their rescue dogs. "She's a family member," Hart says about her rescue dog. "We have our own ugly sweaters so we buy one for her as well."

And cats aren't excluded: at the Crumbs & Whiskers Cat Café, cats in need of forever homes are dressed in their holiday finery in the hopes of being adopted. No doubt the ugly sweaters help draw attention to some pets worthy of good homes!

"Our humans don't have much of a
fashion sense, do they?"

A Catchy Turn of Phrase

Retired Boston Red Sox slugger David Ortiz may have wound up on Santa's naughty list after creating what some might consider an inappropriate Christmas sweater.

Ortiz famously gave an impassioned speech after the Boston Marathon bombings, where he spontaneously exclaimed, "this is our [expletive] city." But naughty word or not, the people of Boston loved it, and Ortiz's words became something of a catchphrase.

So when Ortiz created a Christmas sweater to benefit the David Ortiz Children's Fund, he borrowed from his famous speech. The sweaters feature an image of Ortiz wearing sunglasses and a Santa hat, with the words, "This is our [expletive] Christmas."

Considering that the profits from the slightly profane shirt go to help kids with congenital heart defects, Santa will probably let the naughty shirt slide and keep Ortiz on the nice list.

It's never too early to teach your children
to embrace the ugly sweater tradition.

The Most Wonderful Time of the Year?

A time of happiness, a time of stress, a time of heartwarming actions, a time of mishaps…we close off our book with stories of the ups and downs of the season.

You might just need protective gear to deal with Christmas.

Christmas Injuries

Christmas is one of the happiest times of the year. But did you know it can also be surprisingly—and bizarrely—dangerous? Consider some of these unusual holiday statistics:

Approximately 5,800 Americans are injured every year after falling while hanging holiday decorations. Most of those injuries are the result of falling off ladders, but people have also been known to fall off furniture, stairs, and even rooftops.

Another 5,000 people are treated for electric shocks between Thanksgiving and the New Year, the result of carelessness with Christmas lights and light-up decorations. In fact, in the U.K., dozens of people have died over the last 20 years after watering their Christmas trees with the lights on!

And decorations aren't the only hazards: thousands of people suffer luggage-related injuries every year from hauling oversized bags through crowded airports. And beware those scissors you use to open Christmas packages: 6,000 people need treatment for lacerations every year.

So be smart this holiday season—you don't want to be a statistic!

A Bit of Advice

Sure, sometimes the house looks like a tornado hit after Christmas morning. But listen to Andy Rooney's advice: "One of the most glorious messes in the world is the mess created in the living room on Christmas day. Don't clean it up too quickly."

Lost and Found

Our homes can wind up looking like a tornado swept through after the holidays, so it's hard to blame someone for tidying up. But a mom in the U.K. felt terrible after she cleaned her daughter's room after Christmas in 2016, because she accidentally threw away a card with £200 in gift money.

Lisa Towey didn't realize her daughter Beth's money was gone until after she'd hauled all the trash to the dump. When she got back home, she offhandedly remarked to her daughter that she hoped her Christmas money was in a safe place. Her heart sank when Beth said the money was in a card in her room—the room she'd just cleaned out!

Towey raced back to the dump the next day, and amazingly, workers were able to sift through the huge piles of trash and find Beth's card. "They could have easily just said that it's long gone but they really made an effort," a grateful Towey said.

That Daredevil, Santa

A crowd of one thousand people gathered in Merrymount Park in Quincy, Massachusetts, in 2016 to watch Santa parachute into town. Unfortunately, high winds caused the jolly man to veer off course, and a hard landing resulted in a broken leg. Three elves also leaped from the plane with Santa, and although one of them ended up in a creek, they were all uninjured. EMTs rushed to Santa's aid, and he was transported to a local hospital.

The "Parachuting Santa" is a yearly tradition in Quincy, and is held alongside the city's Christmas Festival Parade. The skydive had already been postponed once due to low clouds. And although observers worried about the windy conditions, the events' organizers decided to go ahead with the jump, telling the crowd that "Santa will do his best."

Perhaps Santa should stick to travelling by sleigh!

**Gift giver. Reindeer wrangler.
Practitioner of extreme sports.**

All's Well That Ends Well

Most of us enjoy leisurely lounging at home on Christmas Day, perhaps watching holiday movies or cooking a big dinner. But residents in the town of Augsburg, Germany, were forced to evacuate on Christmas Day in 2016 for a very important reason: so experts could defuse a 1.8 ton World War II bomb!

The bomb was discovered a week earlier when construction crews were excavating for a parking garage. Instead of immediately evacuating the city, authorities decided to wait until Christmas Day, since there was no imminent threat from the 70-year-old bomb. Christmas Day was deemed the perfect time, since shops are closed, streets are relatively empty, and many people are away with relatives.

Germans also generally hold their biggest Christmas celebration on Christmas Eve, so the inconvenience didn't disrupt festivities. By 7 p.m., the bomb was defused and residents returned to their homes, safe and sound!

Playing Santa

A teenage boy in Valley Stream, New York, was surprised with a Christmas gift from some unexpected givers: the employees of his local Best Buy store.

The boy was a regular at the store, where he'd come in almost every day to play one of the Nintendo Wii U gaming systems. With all of his daily visits, the employees of the Best Buy, including manager Rahiem Storr, got to know the boy and decided to do something special for him for Christmas.

The employees of the store all pitched in and bought the boy his very own Nintendo Wii U, along with a copy of his favorite game, "Super Smash Bros."

"On behalf of all of us here at Best Buy, we got you a Wii U so you don't have to come here every day and play," Storr said in a video that was uploaded to YouTube. What a great example of true Christmas spirit!

Cheer up. Even if your Christmas isn't perfect,
at least you're not being attacked by squirrels.

Christmas Dinner Surprise

Most of us would be rather shocked if we found a gecko in our Christmas dinner broccoli. But 11-year-old Charlie Martin, of Knighton, Wales, was thrilled when his mom found the critter in the vegetables.

Charlie's mom, Jolene, had already chopped up the broccoli on Christmas Eve when she noticed the gecko in the saucepan. Fortunately, the little guy was rescued before the broccoli was cooked!

And Charlie, who only a week earlier had been begging his parents for a gecko, was delighted. The boy already had two turtles, a dog, a bird, fish, and rabbits, but the new gecko—who has been dubbed "Broc"—rounds out his menagerie.

The broccoli was imported from Spain, where the gecko climbed aboard and traveled the hundreds of miles to a Sainsbury's grocery store. A spokesperson for the store said, "Our broccoli is thoroughly inspected and checked while it's being harvested, however this gecko clearly had other ideas and we're glad it's found a new home."

A Friendly Gesture

It's something few employees look forward to: working on Christmas Day. But convenience-store chain vice president Mike Murphy has been working every Christmas Day for more than 40 years.

Murphy, who manages QuickChek stores near the company's Whitehouse Station, New Jersey, headquarters, thinks it's only fair that he show up on the holiday. "If I'm going to have people work that day, then I've always felt I should be there, too," he says.

QuickChek stores are open 24 hours a day, seven days a week. On Christmas Day, Murphy notes that the most popular items sold in the store are cups of coffee and batteries, sometimes purchased by customers still wearing pajamas. But Murphy doesn't mind. In fact, he says it's "fitting as we've been their neighborhood shopping destination all year long."

Murphy, who wears a Santa hat to serve customers their morning coffee, only requires employees to work for four hours on Christmas, and they each receive additional pay.

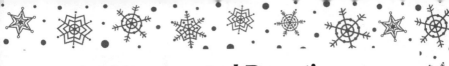

An Unexpected Donation

When we see a familiar Salvation Army bell ringer around the holidays, most of us toss in whatever change we can quickly dig out of our pockets. But one generous benefactor in Sebastian, Florida, gave something much more valuable. Volunteer Jim Bessy was ringing the bell during the 2016 holiday season when an anonymous donor handed him a strange gold coin.

Bessy turned the coin over to Salvation Army Lt. Jay Needham, who discovered that the coin was recovered from a 300-year-old sunken Spanish Galleon, and it was worth thousands of dollars!

Needham said the donation was a welcome gift for the community. "This coin will help bring light on so many stories of families in need," he said.

But this wasn't the first time a Florida Salvation Army kettle received an unusual donation: in 2015, a diamond wedding band was dropped into a kettle in Martin County. (Hopefully on purpose!)